Where Lovers Meet:
Inside the Interior Castle

Where Lovers Meet: Inside the Interior Castle

Susan Muto

ICS Publications
Washington, D. C.
2008

Cover illustration by kind authorization of St. Teresa's Press
© 1982 Carmelite Monastery, Flemington, N.J.

Cover design by Rosemary Moak, O.C.D.S.

ICS Publications
2131 Lincoln Road, NE
Washington, DC 20002-1199
www.icspublications.org

Typeset and produced in the United States of America

Library of Congress Cataloging-in-Publication Data

Muto, Susan Annette.
Where lovers meet : inside the interior castle / Susan Muto.
    p. cm.
Includes bibliographical references.
ISBN-13: 978-0-935216-44-8
1. Teresa, of Avila, Saint, 1515-1582. Moradas. 2. Prayer. I. Title.
BX2179.T4M7265 2007
248.4'82--dc22
                                        2007032478

Contents

Preface and Acknowledgments

There are few spiritual classics as essential to understanding the life of prayer as *The Interior Castle*. Its clarity, order, and beauty are undeniable, yet many readers have asked me to write a "translation" of the translation! I ask them to read this companion text side by side with the *Castle* itself. It is the masterpiece of a mystic whom I consider a personal mentor, of a saint and Doctor of the Church, who has taught–as if she were still here–students the world over, including those who participate in the courses on the mystics and spiritual masters I teach at the Epiphany Academy of Formative Spirituality in Pittsburgh.

When we "meet the masters," we must include in our collection the works of Saint Teresa. Cannot be ignored if we want to understand the difference between mental prayer and recollection, between consolations and spiritual delights, between wordless ecstasy and dwelling on the sacred humanity of Jesus Christ. From the depths of her own experience, amidst awe and bodily ailments, this remarkable author, foundress, and reformer teaches us the essential lessons we need to learn if we hope to enter heaven. She counsels us to listen to the Beloved, to do his will, and to make humility the constant companion of our heart and soul.

Aiding me in bringing this book to publication has been our Epiphany staff with special words of thanks to Maria Muto, who prodigiously typed and retyped every draft, and to Mary Lou Perez, who helped with its final production. I am also deeply grateful to our chaplain-in-residence and senior researcher, Adrian van Kaam, C.S.Sp., Ph.D., who read the manuscript and offered many astute suggestions and refinements. Last but not least, I dedicate this book to our Epiphany friends, associates, and benefactors, who have sustained me in my endeavors to promote formative reading of the Christian classics and whose love for Saint Teresa of Avila has in many cases changed their lives. May she bless us all. May she intercede for our mission and ministry on earth as in heaven, and may her words lead us to need our Beloved with renewed ardor.

Introduction

The edifice Saint Teresa of Avila named *The Interior Castle* offers us a masterful description of divine-human intimacy. This relatively uneducated Spanish woman, who graduated from no theological school, became a mystic, a religious reformer, a renowned spiritual writer, a canonized saint, and a Doctor of the Church. Her spirit permeates the reformed Carmelite movement from its pristine beginnings to the present day. In her convents the nuns still speak of her as if she were in the same room. And so she is, for Madre Teresa lives in the hearts of men and women who sense in her life and works a personal invitation to consecrate their whole being, body, mind, and spirit, memory, intellect, and will, heart and soul, to Christ Jesus our Lord, to Father, Son, and Holy Spirit. No halfway measure will do for this great-souled lover for whom "God alone suffices."

Saint Teresa's personality, like her spirituality, is refreshingly human and wholly humane. She prayed as diligently as she worked, with efficiency and steadfast determination. She was not afraid to express the full range of her feelings. She immersed herself in the physical and emotional trials life demanded of her while placing every person she encountered, every trauma she underwent, and everything she owned in God's hands. Possessing nothing she ended up having all any Christian heart could desire. What longed for was neither bodily comfort nor a heaping on of rewards for the work she did. Her only aspiration was surrender to God. The source of her spirituality, the fountain head of the timeless and timely lessons she teaches us and exemplifies in her life is intimacy with the Trinity. Her daily commitment to trust in His Majesty more than in her own miserable efforts brought Teresa from the depths of self-doubts to the heights of confidence in the Sacred

Humanity and Divinity of Christ. Experience assured her no obstacle is so great that it cannot be overcome by faith in him. In every plan, she looked for God's purpose alone. She was not bewitched by her own skills or expectations. She knew her Spanish honor had to give way to total submission to His Majesty. She realized that the only sure test of the infused graces of contemplative prayer were the fruits of charity that flowed from them.

Her story really begins not in the sixteenth century but in the wilderness near Mount Carmel in the Holy Land. There a small group of devout pilgrims, mostly former crusaders from Europe, searched for a solitary place of prayer where they could share the ideals that drew them together. With utter trust in God and a love for poverty, they organized themselves into a praying community, each one abiding alone in a cave or hut, spending their time in worship and work, leaving their solitude only to join with others for the celebration of the Eucharist. Around 1209, they asked their Bishop, Albert of Jerusalem, to draw up an official code of life based on their practice of the spiritual disciplines in the desert. This code would be their guide and that of all who sought like them to embody these radical Christian ideals. Bishop Albert composed what came to be known as the Primitive Rule of Carmel, a document of twenty-four paragraphs, unpolished yet profoundly edifying. It set forth the path to God for a heart already possessed by him. One is to ponder God's law day and night, obeying his commands while engaging in prayer without ceasing. Even when daily duty compels one's attention, one's heart should to remain at one with God alone.

These hermits of Mount Carmel erected an oratory dedicated to Our Lady. From then until now Carmel has been known as Our Lady's order. Brothers began migrating to Europe around 1239, and, over the next three hundred years, Carmel grew and spread throughout the continent, passing through the manifold ups and downs that mark any religious life in turbulent times. By the sixteenth century, numerous men and women were living in community in accordance with *The Rule of Saint Albert*, though by this time it had witnessed many changes and mitigations.

As this century of transition and searing separation dawned upon Europe, the Christian world was faced with internal crises of dogma and discipline unprecedented in their extent and gravity. The Protestant Reformation was a fact and, by 1545, the Council of Trent had been convoked. It launched the Counter-Reformation, which lasted for many years. Providentially, amidst the social, economic, and political upheavals unleashed by these events, consciousness of the necessity of spiritual transformation struggled to be born anew. Saint Teresa found herself at the heart of this movement of Christian awakening.

She was born in Avila, Spain, during the reign of Ferdinand and Isabella. Her grandfather, a merchant from Toledo in Spain, was a Christianized Jew, who had to move to Avila due to religious pressures. Teresa's father, Don Alonso Sanchez de Cepeda was fourteen when the family arrived there. Alonso married in 1505, but after two years his wife died, leaving him with two children. Four years later he married again, this time to Doña Beatriz de Ahumada, who gave birth on March 28, 1515, to a daughter named after her grandmother. Teresa's mother died at the age of thirty-three, leaving behind her nine other children.

The future saint was a girl of medium height, who tended to be more plump than petite. Her face was round, her forehead broad, her eyes black, lively, and finely placed under thick, dark brows. Her nose was small, her mouth medium in size and delicately shaped, her chin well proportioned, her white teeth equal in size and sparkling. She had three tiny moles, considered a mark of beauty in those days. Her hair was shiny black and curled. In many ways she was an extrovert, cheerful and friendly, a bright conversationalist, bubbling with life.

Only a little girl of seven, she set off with her brother, Rodrigo, for the land of the Moors to have her head cut off for Christ. Fortunately this plan never materialized. With the same undaunted spirit, she played "hermit" with the other children, praying, begging alms, and doing penances.

For some reason, the piety of her youth gave way to a different spirit during her adolescence. She absorbed romantic tales of chivalry, cultivated her feminine charms, planned possibly to marry but soon felt an attraction to the religious life. After her mother's death, when she was twelve years old, she continued to court affection from her cousins, the sons of her aunt, and began a friendship with a frivolous relative. Later she looked back on this period with distaste, having found from experience that one act of humility is worth more than all the knowledge and honor offered by the world. Wishing to free his daughter from such vain company and the enticements it offered, Don Alonso found a good way to do so in 1531 when his oldest daughter married. At the age of sixteen, Teresa was entrusted to the care of the Augustinian nuns of Our Lady of Grace in Avila.

Since there was no public education system in Spain at the time, Teresa probably learned how to read and write at home. Her education in the boarding school did little more than prepare the girls for their future life in marriage, teaching them the usual household skills of cooking, sewing, and the like, complemented by some basic religious instruction. Happily for Teresa, one of her teachers was a woman of deep prayer, who meant more to the young saint than all her former friends. This nun, Doña Maria, loved to talk about God. Her high ideals made Teresa think more seriously about her vocation. The strain of this inner struggle took its toll. She experienced what would be one of many setbacks to her health. She left school to recuperate at her sister's home. Though in time she felt well enough to care for herself, she decided to visit her uncle, Don Pedro, who played a decisive role in her spiritual formation by introducing her to some of the edifying books he relished, one of which helped her to overcome the pressing dilemma she felt over what to do with her life. Reading *The Letters* of Saint Jerome helped her to arrive at a definite decision to follow her vocation to enter the convent.

Unable to bear the thought of separation from his beloved daughter, Don Alonso to give his consent to her becoming a nun. Finally, on November 2, 1535, at the age of twenty, Teresa slipped away from her father's house to give herself to God as a nun in the Carmelite monastery of the Incarnation in Avila. Later, in telling the story of her life, she relates that when she left her childhood home she felt the separation so keenly that she thought she would die. It seemed to her that every bone in her body was torn asunder. A part of her was gone forever, so great was this detachment that it would become a theme of her journey to God at every stage of deepening.

Don Alonso accepted their parting with resignation. He gave his daughter a dowry substantial enough to allow for a modest room of her own in the monastery. Some two hundred persons, including servants and nuns' relatives, were living together at the Incarnation in Teresa's days there. The nuns were required to recite the Divine Office but not to observe enclosure. Days each week were set aside for fasting and abstinence; silence was maintained to encourage a spirit of ceaseless prayer. The Divine Office was celebrated in solemnity and splendor. However, no time was designated for mental prayer. The novices did receive instructions about the Carmelite order, its hermetical origins and its devotion to the Blessed Virgin.

Once again in the autumn of 1538, illness overtook the now professed nun, painful as it was, and again proved to be providential. The doctors could neither determine why she was sick nor find a remedy to cure her. She had to leave the cloister to undergo treatment, but it turned out to be worse than the sickness she endured. For almost three years she became like the paralytic she describes in *The Interior Castle,* losing not only the freedom of mobility but the comfort of feeling understood by others. The best solace she found was in books like *The Morals* of Saint Gregory the Great and best of all Francisco de Osuna's, *The Third Spiritual Alphabet*, which guided her efforts at mental prayer, notably introducing her to the way of recollection.

The young nun threw herself body and soul into the life of religion, attributing her cure to Saint Joseph, her special potion, but still suffering inwardly from the strain brought on by her desire to please God in everything and her growing awareness of sins and distractions caused by following the ways of the world. Out of false humility she almost gave up prayer, a mistake she lamented for the rest of her life more than the fact of her miserable health and an arsenal of other failings.

Though she could function again, Teresa experienced unceasing obstacles to prayer, including a period of dryness lasting for almost eighteen years. This dreadful bout of aridity ended when she received on two occasions in 1554, as though etched on her heart, an image of the wounded Christ that freed her to enter a new path of conversion. Reading *The Confessions* of Saint Augustine, she felt overwhelmed by stirrings of compunction. She received the gift of tears. She lost all trust in herself and placed her life without reservation in the hands of God.

Repentance and relinquishment of self became basic dispositions of her spirituality. Her weeping gave way to joyful ecstasy enkindled by God's splendor. Many a time abject experiences of humiliation turned into songs of jubilation. At the time of her conversion, she became aware of the presence of God in the core of her being. She found that these experiences of inner quiet could not be acquired through her own efforts because they were supernatural. From their onset, a new life began for her. It would culminate in the founding of the Carmelite reform, beginning with the first monastery of Saint Joseph in Avila in 1562 and ending with the writing of *The Interior Castle* in 1577, a few years before her death. The rest of her story would be told in other masterpieces, notably *The Book of Her Life,* written in 1562, and *The Way of Perfection* in 1565.

Once her work of reforming the life of Carmel, in keeping with the original version of *The Rule of Saint Albert,* began in earnest, there was no pause in her mission and ministry until she died. She followed the divine inspiration to establish a small community where she and the nuns who shared her newfound fervor could live in as close a conformity as possible to the first hermits on Mount Carmel. Their life would be devoted to prayer and sacrifice as the best ways of helping their beloved Master and of serving his Bride, the Church.

Teresa's love for Jesus Christ and all members of his body under-girds the enormity of what she wrote and accomplished. This devotion to Trinitarian intimacy was not only the source of her inspiration but the origin of her amazing energy and resourcefulness, her courage and compassion. Together with Saint John of the Cross and others whom she won over to her vision, she persevered in her work with unfailing good humor and unforeseen, indeed unwanted, success, despite the stormy events surrounding her story.

During the remaining years of her life, she founded fourteen convents of Discalced Carmelite nuns, all under incredible duress. With remarkable determination, she introduced the Reform among the Carmelite friars; received the gift of mystical marriage and union with God; and wrote in addition to her other autobiographical and didactic texts, *The Book of Foundations.* This true daughter of the Church died on October 4, 1582, with verses from the Song of Songs on her lips. By then she had already reestablished the Rule of Carmel as a viable way to answer one's religious call in permanent commitment and joyful consecration. Today, more than four hundred years later, thousands of men and women follow her lead, observing the way of life she left as her legacy, and seeing it as the guiding light of their earthly pilgrimage to eternity.

Teresa's personal legacy can be found in the treasury of her books and occasional writings like her *Meditations on the Song of Songs*, composed in 1567. She only picked up her pen when she was close to the age of fifty, after having experienced a steady flow of mystical graces for close to ten years. In *The Book of Her Life*, she was obliged to report in full her inner itinerary so that it could be scrutinized and judged by the ecclesiastical powers to whom she submitted every word.

Because what was happening to her was so remarkable, she found herself having to go from one confessor and spiritual director to another, supplying, when they asked her for it, detailed information about the nature of her prayer. While she readily reported verbally and in writing the account of her sins, the mystical life she was experiencing resisted all attempts to describe it. As she writes in *The Interior Castle*, this search for proper direction was a cross she had to carry not occasionally but most of the time:

> I have had a great deal of experience with learned men, and have also had experience with half-learned, fearful ones; these latter cost me dearly. At least I think that anyone who refuses to believe that God can do much more or that He has considered and continues to consider it good sometimes to communicate favors to His creatures has indeed closed the door to receiving them. Therefore, Sisters, let this never happed to you,

but believe that God can do far more and don't turn your attention to whether the ones to whom He grants His favors are good and bad; for His Majesty knows this, as I have told you. There is no reason for us to meddle in the matter, but with humility and simplicity of heart we should serve and praise Him for His works and marvels.[1]

In addition to her *Life*, Teresa composed several *Spiritual Testimonies*, describing her vocation, her sins, and the graces God gave her. To satisfy the requests of her sisters for a guidebook to mental prayer, she wrote *The Way of Perfection*, revealing to them the threefold path of detachment, humility, and fraternal charity. From then on, the story of her life could be told as a sequence of accomplishments and trials.

In 1567, the General of the Carmelite Order visited Avila and approved the Reform. That same year Teresa founded her second convent at Medina del Campo, where she secured the collaboration of Saint John of the Cross. From 1568 to the year of her death, convents were founded in such places as Pastrana, Toledo, Salamanca, Segovia, Beas, and Seville. In 1573, she wrote *The Book of Foundations* to describe the harrowing yet miraculously happy outcome of her reforming efforts.

Achievements never seemed to occur for Teresa without a crisis. In 1574 her *Life* was denounced to the Inquisition and a year later the General withdrew his approval of the Reform and ordered Teresa back to Castile. Even when things took a turn for the worse, she accepted her trials from the hand of God and never doubted his Providence. She was also convinced that any problems with her new foundations were the work of the devil. He could not endure seeing how faithfully the friars and nuns were serving the Lord. She had no doubt that God permitted these difficulties. Out of such evil he always brought forth great good.

Teresa had only one priority, and that was obedience to the Father's will in conformity to Christ. She vowed to serve him in whatever way he wanted in every event of her life from aridity to rapture. Her trust in the greater good always prevailed. Trials became "precious treasures" given to prepare faithful souls for eternal life. How can we expect the Father to treat those he loves with any less love and sacrifice than he treated his own beloved Son?

Toward the end of her life, exhausted not so much by the brief duration of an ecstasy as by disappointments, intrigues, and troubles, she turned to the only source of strength she had left: His Majesty. For his honor and glory, under obedience, she composed *The Interior Castle*, the crowning work of her life. In it she describes the penultimate stages of the mystical journey to union with God. So inspired was she that she completed this elegant work in a mere two months. Neither trials nor ill health deterred her. She discovered in the course of this writing something she had known all her life–that obedience lessens the difficulty of doing what, humanly speaking, seems impossible. She could not have known in the weak state of health in which she began *The Interior Castle* that it would be a synthesis of her entire spiritual doctrine. In the first chapter she sets forth the tone of her reflections:

> For in reflecting upon it carefully…we realize that the soul of the just person is nothing else but a paradise where the Lord says he finds His delight. So, then, what do you think that abode will be like where a King so powerful, so wise, so pure, so full of all good things takes His delight? I don't find anything comparable to the magnificent beauty of a soul and its marvelous capacity. Indeed, our intellects, however keen, can hardly comprehend it, just as they cannot comprehend God; but he Himself says that he created us in His own image and likeness (IC, 35:1).

The first three dwelling places speak of what is achievable on the way to this paradise if we remain humble. The saint never tires of stressing that human efforts come to naught. We must rely on grace alone. The final four dwelling places deal with the fruits of this receptivity, which comes to full ripeness in the mystical elements of the spiritual life. One of Teresa's early biographers testifies that she told him that on the eve of Trinity Sunday, 1577, that God showed her in a flash the whole book:

> [There was] a most beautiful crystal globe like a castle in which she saw seven dwelling places, and in the seventh, which was the center, the King of Glory dwelt in the greatest splendor. From there he beautified and illumined all those dwelling places to the outer wall. The inhabitants received more light the nearer they were to the center. Outside of the castle all was darkness, with toads, vipers, and other poisonous vermin. While she was admiring this beauty which the grace of God communicates to souls, the light suddenly disappeared and although the King of Glory did not leave the castle, the crystal was covered with darkness and was left as ugly as coal and with an unbearable stench, and the poisonous creatures outside the wall were able to get into the castle. Such was the state of a soul in sin.[2]

In *The Book of Her Life*, Teresa also compares the Divinity to a clear diamond in which everything is visible, including sin with all its deforming effects. Again in the *Life* she describes a moment of mystical vision:

> Once while I was reciting with all the sisters the hours of the Divine Office my soul suddenly became recollected; and it seemed to me to be like a brightly polished mirror, without any part on the back or sides or top or bottom that wasn't totally clear. In its center

Christ, our Lord, was shown to me...I was given understanding of what it is for a soul to be in mortal sin. It amounts to clouding this mirror with mist leaving it black; and thus this Lord cannot be revealed or seen even though He is always present giving us being.[3]

It is clear from these texts that *The Interior Castle* is a forthright expression of Teresa's own experience that the center of the castle is God's dwelling place and that the only way we can enter into its brilliance is through prayer . Though she makes an effort to hide her identity by referring to "this other person she knows," her attempt to conceal the real author was of no avail. Her Christian identity and her feminine spirituality are one. It is Christ who called Saint Teresa to serve his Body, the Church. It is to him that she accorded the fullest honor. It would have been beyond her imagining to conceive that she would be canonized by Pope Gregory XV in 1622 and declared a Doctor of the Church by Pope Paul VI on September 27, 1970. Her only certitude was the depth of her own unworthiness and the fact that her own and our greatest help and blessing resides in turning to him who is the way, the Truth, and the Life (cf. John 14:6). No one can come to the Father save by the Son through the power of the Holy Spirit. Teresa brings to full consciousness the Gospel-directed, Trinitarian-centered, ecclesially-oriented depth of our spirituality. She teaches her sisters and she shows all of us that contemplative union the Trinity is inseparable from an abiding solicitude for the family of God.

Notes

1. Cited in *Teresa of Avila, The Interior Castle*, trans. Kieran Kavanaugh, O.C.D. and Otilio Rodriguez, O.C.D. (New York, Paulist Press, 1979) 89:7. Hereafter abbreviated IC, followed by page and paragraph numbers to this edition.

2. Cited in the Introduction to *The Interior Castle*, 20.

3. Ibid., 21.

Chapter 1
Seeing the Castle for the First Time

The Interior Castle offers a treasury of wisdom for formative reading and reflection on the life of the Spirit. Teresa did not write it in meditative silence but while she was on the move in Toledo, Madrid, Segovia, and Avila. It was not produced in an ivory tower but in the midst of the turmoil of establishing her new foundations. Since she wrote it in accordance with her spiritual state, it expresses her fullest maturity, personally, communally, and religiously.

The year 1577 marked for her a period of struggles, misunderstandings, and crises. Historically, the Carmelite reform had to endure great setbacks despite its enthusiastic start. Saint John of the Cross was in prison. She herself was forced to stay in the monastery in Toledo as if she were in jail. Physically she was so sick and exhausted that her doctors had forbidden her to write. Her own autobiography was in the hands of the Inquisition, making it impossible for her to share it with her sisters.

When her superiors asked her to write about the life of prayer, she complained to her spiritual director, Father Jerome Gracián, that what she had to say was already explained in her *Life* and in *The Way of Perfection*. She was told that since they had no way of quickly referencing what she had recorded there, she was to try to remember the substance of it in another book. She resisted this command, but another confessor intervened and repeated the order that Father Gracián had given her. She then started to write the book as though it were a duplicate of her life story. In practice, it could not be the same because too many other experiences had occurred in her relationships with God and others between 1562 and 1577. Teresa took the path of least resistance as she always did: she obeyed. She writes to her sisters these simple yet profound words:

> The one who ordered me to write told me that the nuns in these monasteries of our Lady of Mount Carmel need someone to answer their questions about prayer and that he thought they would better understand the language used between women, and that because of the love they bore me they would pay more attention to what I would tell them. I thus understood that it was important for me to manage to say something (IC, 34: 4).

Teresa accepted the commission to write the book as a testimony to the efficacy of obedience. From a subjective point of view she claims that she started its composition with no inspiration whatsoever. She did it because she was obliged to do so for the sake of her sisters:

> Not many things that I have been ordered to do under obedience have been as difficult for me as is this present task of writing about prayer. First, it doesn't seem that the Lord is giving me either the spirit or the desire to undertake the work. Second, I have been experiencing now for three months such great noise and weakness in my head that I've found it a hardship even to write concerning necessary business matters (IC, 33:1).

Any of us, faced with a task we felt incapable of performing, would feel the same way:

> Indeed, I don't think I have much more to say than what I've said in other things they have ordered me to write about will be nearly all alike. I'm, literally, just like the parrots that are taught to speak; they know no more than what they hear or are shown, and they often repeat it (IC, 33:1).

Here we find a touching image of who a spiritual writer like Teresa is and of what she may become as an instrument of the Divine. Everything seems to be against the task of readying this book, yet she does it. She plunges into its composition as if she is under the impetus of an irresistible force of grace. As we read in the First Dwelling Places:

> Today while beseeching our Lord to speak for me because I wasn't able to think of anything to say nor did I know how to begin to carry out this obedience, there came to my mind what I shall now speak about, that which will provide us with a basis to begin with. It is that we consider our soul to be like a castle made entirely out of a diamond or of very clear crystal, in which there are many rooms, just as in heaven there are many dwelling places (IC, 35:1).

Out of this inspired comparison emerges one of the most profound mystical works ever transcribed on paper. How is it possible to have achieved such an outcome? Biographers and commentators say that the book was written in a sudden burst of inspiration and that it is a synthesis of what Teresa had learned through her earlier life in the Reform and her reading of both secular and sacred books. Almost as if she were writing a "story of a soul," Teresa chose three subplots that together form the main pillars of this masterpiece: 1) *The Castle*—which becomes a symbol of the paradise within; 2) *The Lady*—who is the soul; and 3) *The Knight*—who is God. In a complementary fashion, three main convictions seem to uphold the castle walls. They are: 1) that God is present in the soul; 2) that the soul is the continual recipient of divine graces; and 3) that God helps us to overcome sin and to communicate directly with him through prayer.

Teresa experienced the awesome and humbling truth that the soul is God's dwelling place. We are as capable of enjoying him as is the crystal of reflecting the light of the sun. Grace illumines our interiority like a diamond refracts the entire spectrum of light. It pierces through the hard crust of sin like a laser beam. Teresa experiences any missing of this mark as a thick, black darkness. To communicate with God as an intimate friend is impossible if this stain is not wiped away by penance and unceasing prayer. Because of the friendship that already exists between God and us by virtue of our creation, its loss is catastrophic.

The masterful touch Teresa brings to these profound theological truths is always descriptive and formative, not abstract and speculative. Each expression of faith comes from experience. Each virtue gains in credibility thanks to a concrete image, symbol, or metaphor with which we can identify. The coherence of Teresa's thought matches the depth of her own soul searching. It is nothing short of miraculous how little time it took her to write *The Interior Castle*. Her spiritual director, Father Gracián, arrived in Toledo and gave her his instructions on May 29, 1577. On May 30 and 31, her confessor intervened to support what he said and then purchased writing materials for her. On June 1 and 2, she wrote the Prologue. From June 3 to 17, she completed the first four dwelling places. There was a brief interruption from June 18 until the end of October, including the death of the Papal Nuncio whose funeral she had to attend. Then she traveled the remainder of the month to Toledo, Madrid, and Segovia. En route she wrote the Fifth Dwelling Places. She returned to Avila in November and finished the book in less than four weeks for a total of two months of composition.

In every line of *The Interior Castle*, Teresa invites us to participate in the graced action that occurs between us and God through prayer. She also insists on the strict coherence between the life of virtue and the quest for intimate conversation with the One who loves us. Asceticism and mysticism converge in a higher synthesis: the direct experience of

God's presence in the soul and in its epiphanic manifestations in the world. The spiritual life is a two-fold process, ascetical and mystical. The ascetical life of purifying formation and illuminating reformation underpins the mystical life of unifying transformation. This higher state of union and communion guards against any excesses in the ascetical realm, including the erratic exercise of self-imposed mortifications. Each of the dwelling places respects this twofold process, insisting that discipline in moderation and the intimacy of fruitful discipleship are inseparable from one another.

The message Teresa communicates is at once literal and symbolic, starting with the allegory of the castle itself. It is both a seat of war, with moats surrounding it and foes trying to enter, and a sign of peace, with the diamond-like crystal of the soul in love with Christ at its center. Without this struggle we would make no progress on the way of perfection. Enemy forces would try to pull us away from the interior of the castle where God dwells. In this battle zone, grace protects us and draws us to the immortal diamond of divine love. The terror of purgative struggles and the tenderness of illuminative breakthroughs must both be endured for Christ's sake. The ammunition of sin tempts us to run from the action of grace, but we need not fear. As our guide assures us, the attraction of sin dims to nothingness in comparison to the light of Christ.

Chapter 2
Stepping Across the Threshold

Many and varied are the dwelling places in this castle where contemplation and action converge. In the center, at a depth only God knows, an encounter like no other occurs. The entryway to this deepest place of grace is prayer. It teaches us that anything less than the love of God in our souls is not worth pursuing. Our focus should be on our longing for union with him alone. Surrounding the castle are ditches and moats filled with many reptiles. These slimy creatures represent the seductive temptations to become preoccupied with substitutes for the transcendent. Our body is likened to a fence because inside of it rages a battle between the graced actions of God and the self-centered, idolatrous leanings of our fallen nature. Surrounding the castle are courtyards full of debris that image the unredeemed world and all in it that pulls us away from Christ.

Teresa's description of the castle reflects not the black and white of static information but in full color of ecstatic transformation. Words gush forth like waterfalls to capture something of that continual penetration of grace in the inmost chambers of our interiority where the mystery of God's initiative toward us is unceasing. His beloved Son is the knight, who tirelessly appeals to our heart and invites us to enter into the center of the bridal chamber, to seek the light shining from the diamond of our divinized calling in him.

The bride-soul is free to choose which way to take. As she approaches the awesome edifice where the knight lives, she has to decide. Will she remain outside its portals in the ditches, fighting with her foes? Will she venture across the threshold of the castle and come under the protection of the knight? His intention is clear: union with her soul, but his way is appealing not coercive. It is her move now. Does she have the courage to open the door and penetrate into the depths of this divine dwelling? Will she stay on the outskirts, risking encounter with the formidable foe of her own sinfulness accompanied by the fatal blows of demonic seduction? If she does not make the right decision, will she be subject to condemnation or is this battle a necessary chapter in the diary of her salvation?

The inner struggle of the soul with sin is one side of this divine-human tension; the other consists of God's continual drawing of her toward himself. The first step on the way to our becoming spiritually mature has to be a passion to please God and a promise to rely on his grace. Once our self-will surrenders to Christ, we are able to let go of all other preoccupations and enter the First Dwelling Places. Even on the lowest floor of the castle, we are inside! Once there, the action of deepening under the impact of grace begins in earnest. If we hesitate to pass through that first portal, we may lose the courage to explore the castle and all of its chambers. The initial choice to cross the threshold presupposes a longing to reach its center. As Teresa says:

> …we are speaking to other souls that, in the end, enter the castle. For even though they are very involved in the world, they have good desires and sometimes, though only once in a while, they entrust themselves to our Lord and reflect on who they are, although in a rather hurried fashion (IC, 38-39, 8).

This glimmer of reflection is not enough to tell us what the Lord ultimately asks of us. We are still too preoccupied with our own affairs to place his will first. Teresa is honest about this fact of life:

> During the period of a month [such souls] will sometimes pray, but their minds are then filled with business matters that ordinarily occupy them. They are so

attached to these things that where their treasure lies
their heart goes also. Sometimes they do put all these
things aside, and the self-knowledge and awareness
that they are not proceeding correctly in order to get
to the door is important. Finally, they enter the first,
lower rooms. But so many reptiles get in with them
that they are prevented from seeing the beauty of the
castle and from calming down; they have done quite a
bit just by having entered (IC, 39:8).

Finding the paradise within requires passing over, with our attention fixed on God, moats filled with reptiles and other vermin.
Once inside the castle, we can breathe a sigh of relief, knowing that
the journey to transformation has begun in earnest. From the start we
learn a lesson we will never forget. If we forfeit the graced opportunity to mature in Christ, if we opt not to go forward because of our
attachments to outer preoccupations and the lack of a reflective life,
we may miss the best chance we have to discover who we are and who
God wants us to become. If we stay outside the castle walls, we may
never experience the joys that await those who choose to plunge into
its depths. The starting point of this journey to union with God is the
truth of God's indwelling in our soul, of his nearness, and intimacy,
of his self-communication to us through unconditional love and compassion. Every time we pray, we acknowledge God's presence in our
hearts while allowing this gift to expand in efficacy in all our works.

Each dwelling place respects this basic need of ours to return home
to God despite the obstacles that stand in our way. Each represents
a degree or intensity of grace, a stopover in the process of the inter-
penetration of our inmost self by God. Each level guides us to new
depths of self-knowledge to be found nowhere else in no other way.
As each veil is drawn away from the crystal or the diamond that we
are, a new phase of Christian maturation is attained. Teresa identifies

seven veils that need to be progressively removed if we hope to pass from one mansion to the next. In so many words they are:

1. Deliberate sin. Mortal sin, being the thickest darkness, has absolutely no place on this journey. It crushes the crystal clarity Christ intends for our soul. It must be submitted to the healing power of his grace.

2. Detachment from external affairs. To the degree that they preoccupy us, they prevent us from attaining, in response to God's call, the grace of interior recollection. Our minds are like racing cars speeding around narrow tracks. We are not able for more than a moment to come to that inner stillness in which we may hear the shy whispers of the Holy Spirit.

3. Hidden defects. Thanks be to the grace of God, we have been freed from their seductive power, but their remnants still cling to us like barnacles on a sunken ship.

4. Detachment from the intellect. No matter how much we, with our reasoning powers, think we know God, we need to let go of our ideas and assumptions about God so that we can really begin to dwell with the mystery of the Trinity in the core of our being.

5. Detachment from the will. No matter how much we say we love God, we need to examine the tight grip self-centered willfulness or lazy willessness has upon us. Then we can begin to attach our love-will to the Divine Will.

6. Detachment from sentiments or feelings on the affective level. Unless this letting go occurs, we will be unable to experience tranquility of soul in both consolation and desolation, in calm and storm, with equal love and equal forgetfulness.

7. Detachment from either great suffering or great joy. Equanimity and complete effacement of our ego are the most reliable passageways from purgation to illumination to union with God.

To reclaim this deeply the Christ-form of our soul demands detachment on all levels of the self: sociohistorical, vital, functional,
and transcendent. All inordinate attachments have to be replaced by
dispositions of surrender to God. To come to this liberating plane of
love, we need to peel away, in cooperation with grace, the seven veils
that keep us from union with our Beloved in the interior castle. This
removal happens through a progressive process of heartfelt purification
as we pass from mansion to mansion.

In her humility, Teresa realizes that simply asking for these graces
does not guarantee that we will receive them. We feel her struggle
within ourselves as we follow the grace that has gone before us to bring
us to this point on our mystical journey. She makes us acutely aware
of the turmoil the soul goes through. In the process of taking off these
veils and slowly negating their power to obscure the diamond's light,
we discover how powerless we are. The initiative for transformation
belongs wholly to God. Our openness to his love outpoured through
the Spirit has a forming and transforming effect on our soul. It arouses
in us waves of serenity, equilibrium, tranquility, and peace. All of these
gifts alert us to the pushes and pulls that tear our life apart outside of the
castle while arousing in us a longing to be within its walls. Beckoning
us to safety, but never to complacency, is the presence of Christ in our
soul.

This struggle and the dynamics of radical detachment associated with it comprise the ascetical side of our sojourn in these First
Dwelling Places. Awareness of the power of grace and the infused
self-communications of God comprises the mystical side of this story.
Summarizing this interplay so far we see that:

1. Each dwelling place bestows on us a special favor of God that
    helps us to enter that section of the interior castle. No matter how
    valiant our ascetical efforts may be, were it not for the grace of

God we could not even take the first step, leading to the lowest chamber of these amazing mansions.

2. Each of them sustains us in our practice of some old and new methods of prayer. They represent our answers to God's initiative, stretching from rudimentary intercessions to the farthest reaches of wordless worship.

3. Each mansion we enter draws us to a more sincere expression of our moral and ethical commitments. Gospel truths attract us as we move from superficial to substantive floors of the castle. Mystical growth in spirituality can only be trusted if it rests on the solid foundation of Christian morality. How else can the Gospel make a difference in our daily life and in our dealings with the world? Teresa offers us this sober word of caution. As our journey continues, she begs us to stay on guard:

> If a person is to enter the second dwelling places, it is important that he strive to give up unnecessary things and business affairs. Each one should do this in conformity with his state in life. It is something so appropriate in order for him to reach the main dwelling place that if he doesn't begin doing this I hold that it will be impossible for him to get there. And it will even be impossible for him to stay where he is without danger even though he has entered the castle, for in the midst of such poisonous creatures one cannot help but be bitten at one time or another (IC, 45-46, 14).

Chapter 3
Entering the Doors

Having entered the portals of the First Dwelling Places, we cannot help but wonder what favors God has in store for us? What is the initiative our Beloved intends to take? What is the degree of intensity of grace? The shimmering awareness of God's indwelling presence, like the glow of light at the end of a tunnel, intrigues and attracts us. Despite how preoccupied we may be with external affairs, God gives us a glimpse of what awaits faithful servants and friends who are not so busy about being busy that they forget his presence. This disclosure may come when we least expect it—while reading a book, conversing with a companion, walking alone under the stars. Suddenly our life changes. We cannot return to where we were, but neither do we know what lies ahead. We feel afraid, but we must have faith.

In these Dwelling Places the first favor granted to us by God is the calming of our fears. Strong as the terrifying awareness of our own alienating sinfulness may be, stronger still is the assurance of his presence within us. There is no use hiding our attachments from him any more. The Spirit invites us to name our idols and smash them, to cease lying to ourselves and defending our mistakes. In compunction of heart, we sense that we are literally inhabited by God. We can no longer ignore the truth that His Majesty stoops to embrace our misery. How pitiful our persistent forgetfulness of who we really are now seems. We only exist because we belong in essence to God. How could we be so blind to the self-knowledge revealed to us by our Beloved? What powers so plague us that they cause us to resist his gracious claim upon us?

In Chapter One of the First Dwelling Places, Teresa suggests a number of reasons why this kind of formation ignorance cancels recognition of our transcendence dynamic. Blinded to our deepest identity, oblivious to the Christ-form of our soul, we live like bats bound to dark caves when all the while God gives us wings to fly under the sun. The main reason for this sad condition is our clinging to lesser "gods"— to power, pleasure, and possession, to fame, notoriety, and prestige instead of casting our lot with the grandeur of God. The obstacles that stand in the way of our progress in this first stage of our journey are formidable. It is as if we focus all of our concerns on what lies outside of the castle. This sign of status, that momentary gratification, these collectibles we amass are what fill our minds and clutter our hearts. Inside the castle, at its very center, God awaits in pristine simplicity for our coming while we run aimlessly hither and yon. Now it seems as if God's waiting upon us becomes more urgently eager for our response. He has taken the initiative to give us first the awareness of our reliance on him; then, despite our unworthiness, he seems to want our company. If only for a moment, our preoccupations with the outside world, our battles with our foes and all that fills the moats around the castle, cease to attract our attention. We begin to question our hesitation to change, but we need more direction.

Chapter Two has a didactic intention. Teresa wants us to learn once and for all that not to enter the castle is to risk living in continual sinfulness, groping for light when it is ours for the asking. What a loss it is to miss the chance to communicate with the one Person who truly understands and loves us. No wonder we feel so unhappy. The crushing blow dealt to our deceptive existence must be administered by humility. It is the key virtue that unlocks the prison doors that prevent our walk to freedom. It instills in us both the fear of offending God and the realization that any good thing we are or do has its source in his truth. As Teresa says with both authority and clarity:

> For never, however exalted the soul may be, is anything else more fitting than self-knowledge; nor could it be even were the soul to so desire. For humility, like the bee making honey in the beehive, is always at work. Without it, everything goes wrong. But let's remember that the bee doesn't fail to leave the beehive and fly about gathering nectar from the flowers. So it is with the soul in the room of self-knowledge; let it believe me and fly sometimes to ponder the grandeur and majesty of its God. Here it will discover its lowliness better than by thinking of itself, and be freer from the vermin that enter the first rooms, those of self-knowledge. For even though, as I say, it is by the mercy of God that a person practices self-knowledge, that which applies to what is less applies so much more to what is greater, as they say. And believe me, we shall practice much better virtue through God's help than by being tied down to our own misery (IC, 42-43:8).

Here our mentor cautions us not to focus so much on our own lack of wholeness lest we lose sight of the horizon of the Holy. What she suggests is that in seeking to know who we are we need to soar aloft in meditative reflection on the redemptive mercy of God best revealed in the cross of Christ. Let that be our focus, not our failings. In this light we will be able to penetrate to a profounder level of self-knowledge, rooted in the person-to-Person relationship that exists between us and God. Teresa offers excellent counsel in this regard for beginners in prayer. Because we feel the weight of our own unworthiness, we face the danger of being encapsulated in anxious introspectionism, false guilt feelings, and self-condemning scrupulosity. Teresa reminds us that compunction of heart must be accompanied by remembrance of

God. The advice she gives is of vital importance to anyone attempting to make progress in the life of the Spirit. In essence we are to imitate Christ: despising sin but loving and forgiving sinners, starting with ourselves. This orientation toward transcendent self-presence reminds us in the throes of self-centered introspectionism that God is with us, that we are never alone, and that, in the words of Jesus, "...anyone who comes to me I will never drive away (John 6:37).

Each Dwelling Place, we recall, has a two-fold approach: on the one hand, the mystical pull of God; on the other hand, the ascetical attempts we make to respond to grace to choose not our own will but God's will for us. In the first mansion this mystical attraction consists in our catching a glimpse of the mystery of love that sustains and embraces our essence and existence. This renewed awareness of who God is and of who he invites us to be gives rise to a rudimentary way of prayer that is our answer to the awesome reality of the divine initiative. It does not consist of a lofty state of ecstasy but in a flicker of awareness that lets us feel the welling up of pure wonder. A sigh or a groan might be all we can muster. These breaths are brief but intense and pertinent to the soul's progress. They signify that we do have a sense of who it is to whom we must pray and of what it is for which we ought to ask. These movements, however pedestrian they may seem, mark the start of much deeper forms of prayer.

On the ascetical side of cooperation with grace, we begin to acknowledge what has to happen if we are not to lose the blessings that accompany such moments of reflective awareness. No longer can we deny that living in sin of any sort is a serious concern or that being absorbed in worldly affairs mars reflection. We are puffed up with the need for honors and ambitions, engulfed in selfish pleasures, careless about our progress in prayer. We admit that our communication with

God is much too infrequent and that, as a result, we are unable to find lasting peace.

Although we see to our horror the snakes and vipers that surround us, we must admit that in this ascetical struggle there is also much to appreciate. A true gift is the emergence of higher longings and purer intentions. We want to reform our dissonant dispositions; we long to love God more. Good desires spark just noticeable improvements in the exchanges between us and our Beloved. They reveal no quantum leaps in our life of prayer, but they are positive complements of the negative awareness that we are swamped in sin and desperately in need of redemption.

The symbols Teresa draws upon in the First Dwelling Places highlight this tension. The paralytic man is likened to the soul at this juncture of the journey. Without repentance we are like persons whose limbs are paralyzed. We possess hands and feet, but we cannot move or control them. Ours is a disordered existence, without rhyme or reason. Our arms and legs go one way, our head and heart another. Our whole being feels fragmented. Other symbols offset the use of this central image that cripples everything. Teresa speaks of the soul in the state of grace as an oriental pearl. She consoles us with the welcome news that even in the heart of such paralyzed persons resides this pearl, if only it can be discovered. In the inmost core of the paralytic, as in the core being of the chained-captive and the deaf-mute, there is a lovely jewel in which God takes delight. This is the *Imago Dei*, the image of God in us.

The question that begs to be answered is this: Why ought we to remain paralyzed and stuck in sin when God wants us to arise and walk? Teresa shares her conviction that there is no reason for us to be in this prison of our own making. We can swim past our foes, cross the moat, and enter the castle. Our body itself will become the setting for this diamond. It will be the protective outer wall that keeps the crystal from becoming chipped or fragmented. As we dare to approach the castle, we are stunned to see that God himself meets us at the door. We are dying of thirst and he leads us to the springs of life we seek.

Teresa's teaching at this early stage exposes us to the phasic nature of the interior life. She helps us to discover where we are on our spiritual journey. The main work we are to do in response to grace is to attune our lives to the will of the Father and to remain faithful to the teachings of the Church. Without humility and obedience, the other virtues of the spiritual life cannot possibly unfold. We must not be overly concerned about the future. Any such anxiety is unnecessary if we learn to trust God now and to accept what Holy Providence allows in our daily situation. We do not need to do extraordinary acts of mortification to prove our good will. Superb spiritual teacher that she is, Teresa knows how to call the fears of simple souls like us. We may not be able to absorb intellectually the amount of analysis behind these spiritual stages, but we respond well to her plea for moderation. She gives us the courage and candor we need to confess with our whole being that we want nothing more than to live in greater intimacy with God.

Chapter 4
Going Past These Portals

God's whisper is enough to encourage our searching soul to aspire to enter the Second Dwelling Places. The favor God wants to grant us now is a firmer letting go of what is ultimately unimportant—our plans, our projects, our personal, social, and ecclesial concerns. What matters at this juncture of the journey is that we recover, at least from time to time, the interior quiet that readies us to do God's will in as detached and non-distracted a way as possible. There are tasks to which we must attend in accordance with our vocation, but how we do so is what concerns Saint Teresa. Can we hear the shy hints the Spirit sends to let God be God in our life and to let go of our own agendas or do we allow unnecessary stresses, tensions, and preoccupations to deface our inner peace?

Teresa's sense of timing in this mansion is brilliant. Her counsels convince us that we need to be aware of when to retire inwardly, even if only for a few moments, to hear the Spirit's call. Distractions attack us at every turn. Unless we regain proper perspective and give priority to God, we may not be able to pass through the next set of portals and come closer to the core of the castle.

Many battles besiege the soul at this turning point. She feels torn between worldly affairs, symbolized by vipers, and God's persistent invitation. Her dilemma concerns a double attraction: to do what has to be done to fulfill her calling and simultaneously to rest in and wait upon the Lord's bidding in the inner depths of her soul. She is not mature enough in her spiritual life to reconcile contemplation and action so the tug of war continues. Teresa calls these external attractions vipers because they grab at us erratically, draining our spiritual stamina like leeches suck out life's blood. Their sole purpose is to tempt us away from our inmost calling in Christ. It does not cease to call us despite the imbalance of our present existence.

The viper's trick is to deceive us into thinking that temporal affairs escalate in significance to the point where they almost seem the eternal. They try to deceive us into believing that worldly success will grant us at some point ultimate satisfaction. This illusion blinds us to the inherent finitude of earthbound affairs. However splendid our accomplishments may be. Their outcomes pass away over time if we do not give the credit to God. The way of the vipers is to hold before our mind's eye the esteem in which the world holds us when we exercise this kind of activism. They make us secretly relish people's praise. Our pride-form allures us into thinking that our worthwhileness rests on the works in which we are engaged rather than in the God we serve. These clever devils also try to convince us that any kind of withdrawal to worship God in solitude is a big mistake. What will the other "worker bees" think of us if we take time to "Be still and know that I am God" (Psalm 46:10).

Vipers, generally speaking, symbolize the modes of self-deception that take us away from our interior call to meet God with utter candor, as Teresa did. On the other side of this tug of war is the Spirit, who never ceases to send through the channels of our transfocal consciousness divine inspirations to assist us in discerning the illusory tricks the vipers try to play. The weapons we have at our disposal to combat them are our intellect, memory, and will. Properly used in conjunction with grace, these faculties help us to see through and rise above the most subtle deceptions our egocentricity can devise.

His Majesty appeals to all the powers of reflection with which we are endowed by our Creator. However attached we may be to temporal goods, we know in our hearts they have no eternal value. They cannot bestow lasting benefits on our soul unless we live in poverty of spirit, always mindful of how much we owe to God. Reason compels us to attend to our finitude while faith tells us that God created us for blessings beyond measure. The vipers howl with cackles of glee when we boast that we are self-made persons. There is no such creature on earth.

To walk in the truth of who we are is to admit that our days are numbered. Inner peace eludes us if are ashamed of our creaturehood or try to hide it. The paradise we seek lies within the castle, not at its outer rim. Kingdoms fall. Pleasures fade. Possessions gather dust. In this sobering light of humility, to whom can we cling but Christ? A parent dies. A best friend goes away. An apostolate to which we dedicated so much energy folds up. In a moment of truth, we take a long, retrospective look at our own lives and on all those who have preceded us through these portals of time. How soon their possessions are forgotten! All that we hold dear is from the start a gift of God to us, but even the best gifts only last for a certain period. God alone never leaves us, never betrays our trust. With renewed clarity we see the portals leading to the interior path, our of reach of the siren song of the vipers. The infused theological virtues of faith, hope, and love orient us to the chief priority we ought to pursue: to love God and seek his company, "so much that from time to time He calls us to draw near Him" (IC. 49:2). The rest of our life flows from this relationship.

The tension the soul feels when she crosses from the land of illusion to the door of truth is excruciating. Having been there herself, Saint Teresa assures us that only sober reality checks will free us from the burdensome weight of self-deception. In line with the teaching of Saint John of the Cross—that self-renunciation is the key to inner and outer liberation—Teresa, too, says: "Embrace the cross" with joy, knowing that "perfect love casts out fear" (1 John 4:18). For both saints, there is no better shield against the lies by which we live than the timber of the cross. Souls capable of the greatest suffering because of their identification with Christ enjoy the greatest freedom. At this crossover phase between self-sufficiency and dependence on God, the pull between exteriority and interiority becomes more fierce. What causes this tension to worsen? On the one hand, the worldliness of the world beckons us to cave in to its secularistic ideal of human greatness rather than to embrace the humility of sanctified and sacrificial service. On the other hand, the Word of God whispered within our hearts invites us to leave the Egypts of our bondage, crush the idols of our own self-importance, and cross the desert of doubt to the promised land of our divine calling. We may suffer much humiliation from this awakening, but only in this way can we regain our freedom.

The kinds of questions we ask ourselves during blessed pauses for reflection reveal how much we want to be released from the dissipating superficiality of a self-centered spirituality. There is no quick fix for this debilitating condition. Piling on more external customs, more structures, rules, and regulations is not the answer either. Our struggle is not exterior but interior. With all the baggage we carry, it is no wonder we feel overburdened. Now is the time to take off our overloaded knapsacks and walk more freely into the rest rooms of the castle. Once we refresh our fatigued interiority at the wellspring of divine grace, we may again be ready to give our all to the people we serve. In these early stages of divine transformation, we do not yet see how we can reconcile the side of our life committed to solidarity with this inner longing for solitude.

Our restlessness now becomes the catalyst that moves us toward a more reflective stance. Surely time and eternity need not feel so severed from one another. The fact that this struggle continues in souls on the way to spiritual deepening is a good sign that grace is at work. Moments of spiritual insight come upon us more frequently than in the past. At the end of the day, we wish we had spent less time focusing on our gains and losses and more time in remembrance of God.

If we do not progress much further than this point of recognition of our utter inadequacy without a personal relationship with God, we have taken a bigger step toward appraising the true nature of our call, vocation, and avocation than we may think. By paying attention to the Spirit-illumined invitation to rest in God before we act, we are more ready, when the time comes, to be "Christ bearers." We bring the blessings of these solitary moments of dwelling in our Father's house with us wherever we go and whatever we do. What ceases are the kinds of preoccupations typical of persons overly bound to their own climb up the ladder of success to positions of greatness contrary to the Gospel truth that "He must increase, but I must decrease" (John 3:30).

In this section and throughout *The Interior Castle*, progress occurs according to a two-fold process: *mystical* (the pull of God drawing us toward prayer and meditation) and *ascetical* (the gentle efforts we are called to make under the impetus of grace to facilitate this sacred journey). Never must our desire to grow be cut off from this divine initiative. Most of us in the modern world have been educated by the mentality that we can do by ourselves alone whatever has to be done. We can reform bad habits if we try harder. We can transform our social, familial, organizational, and ecclesial lives. In short, we live in the illusion that we can reach high planes of self-perfection without God's help. After that we may turn to him with a perfunctory word of thanks and ask him to bless our efforts! We confuse the gentle, cooperative bending of our will toward God's will with a strong ego drive that says we must practice excessive penances, undergo erratically heroic mortifications, and subject ourselves to extraordinary suffering, so that we can prove to God that our ascetical efforts in mind by themselves alone make us worthy to receive the graces he freely grants. We forget that the dispensations of the Divine are not our doing. Our prayer life grows or regresses according to how well we respond to God's ever-present graciousness, not to the clever projects of personal or communal salvation we devise.

Prayer understood in Teresa's terms as conversation with the One who loves us is a response to God's self-communications to us. The mystical pull of God at this stage of castle dwelling draws us to a deeper level of listening associated with rudimentary or vocal prayer, complemented by meditation. The soul is no longer deaf to God's call. Intellect, memory, and will are activated in the direction of the Divine through meditative reflection. God speaks to our soul in many ways. The timid whispers of the Spirit may come to us through the teachings and example of good people, through sermons, and the reading of holy books. God also appeals to us to yield to him in appreciative abandonment to the mystery in events not under our control like natural disasters, physical illness, and spiritual trials. The truths the Spirit teaches us at various times in our lives may be difficult to digest, but we cannot ignore their efficacy. Gentle yet firm perseverance on our part, the ascetical approach, aims at our becoming less sufficient unto ourselves and more reliant on God's way with us. The tension that once tore our heart in two lessens when we see the difference between where we were and where God wants us to go. To verbalize this distinction is not easy because it means admitting into awareness the faults we still recognize in ourselves. Yet now dissonance becomes not a rift to deny, but a call to greater consonance with Christ as we confess:

1. As much as I wish to do so, I do not always avoid the occasions of sin that separate me from you, my Lord…

2. I still have many fears.

3. I am unable to find peace.

4. I feel more fragmented than whole.

5. I harbor a great deal of confusion and doubt in regard to where you want to lead me.

6. I do not know if I have the courage to take up my cross and follow you to death's door. (Luke 14:27)

Honest expressions like these can pose a danger if we allow them to degenerate into excuses for scrupulosity and harsh self-judgment, lacking gentleness toward ourselves and others. It is important for us to shift from this negative stance to a more positive awareness of one of the loving Providence of God. However profound our misery may be, it never diminishes the divine mercy God wants to give us. Rather than engaging in debilitating self-abasement, we need to remember his call and respond humbly and patiently to it. Positive reminders of where we want to be might be expressed as follows:

1. Though I feel unworthy of your friendship, Lord, I believe that you are with me in your risen glory. You really care about me.

2. I accept despite my flaws that you have made me an immortal diamond, reflecting your glory.

3. I know that you want to be with me, asking only that I trust you on all levels of my bodily, mental, emotional, and spiritual make-up.

4. As you allow my intellect, memory, and will to become more alert to your will, I welcome chances to let go of my sleepy taken-for-grantedness. I celebrate more frequently the graces you send me in splendid infusions of humility, detachment, and charity.

The suffering associated with growth in the knowledge of who we are can be traced in many instances to coercive dispositions that stand in the way of peaceful surrender to our life in God and God's life in us. Teresa consoles us by saying that His Majesty is in no hurry.

He will wait for an eternity, if necessary, for us to enter the castle. We must not expect this intimate encounter to happen overnight. This awareness of God's waiting for us and watching over us fills us with such wonder that we can no longer resist the Spirit's urging. We leap over these outer moats and lean on the counsels Teresa gives us:

1. Fraternize with faithful companions, who are also desirous of deepening their spiritual life by moving closer to the center of the castle.

2. Do not count up, as you would buttons in a sewing kit, the spiritual favors God may grant to you. A calculative mentality erodes, it does not build up this spiritual edifice! Do not rely on consolations as if they were sure signs of God's favor. They may only be dreams of your own making or indicators that you are trying too willfully to offset God's crucifying gift of aridity.

3. Be ready to resist the attacks of the vipers, but do so carefully. Be aware that you are not alone in this struggle. There is no speed-track to this place of grace, no instant technique to arrive at the center of the castle.

4. Simply carry on and do not lose heart. This is the way to achieve inner peace. Live always in a hopeful state of presence. Remember that discouragement can hinder or halt your spiritual progress. Replace it by instant appreciative abandonment.

5. When you feel yourself losing ground, be ready to consult wise guides, learned and experienced in these matters.

Saint Teresa obliged herself to seek spiritual direction because the favors she received were so unnerving. She had to be sure they were of God, but she was not as well understood by certain guides as she would have liked to be. That is why she makes such a point to be a good spiritual teacher herself. Although she had been scarred by improper counsel, she never used it as an excuse to block the movements of God in her soul.

Having passed through the Second Dwelling Places, it is safe to say that our move onward in the spiritual life has begun to pick up a bit of speed. Progress is thoroughly dependent on our past experiences of grace and on what God has in store for us in the future. Still nothing is lost on the path to maturity in the Lord. All that happens to us is integrated, expanded, and enhanced by the power of the Holy Spirit. We must never feel, as we are led by the mystery from the Second to the Third Dwelling Places, that now we are through with meditation and previous forms of prayer. Nothing could be farther from the truth. All we have learned goes with us, only its fruits are increasingly refined.

Chapter 5
Inside the Castle

The intensity of grace granted in the Third Dwelling Places advances our spiritual life by enabling us to persevere in our commitment to give priority to God. Teresa expresses this thought when she says that: "Through perseverance and the mercy of God we have won these battles and have entered the rooms of the third stage" (IC. 55:1). All other attachments unwittingly placed by us before His Majesty pale in comparison. There is no doubt in our minds that we have been overly attached to external matters, but of what use is it to forfeit the good we have gained by failing to be aware of the difference between temporal means and eternal ends.

This special favor of persevering in the life of the Spirit is not like a feat for which we take credit; it requires a true leap of faith. So favorably disposed is God's toward the good will we show that he grants us the inner strength and the courage we need to continue our journey despite the obstacles strewn on our path. In the second phase of faith deepening, we focused on the struggle that goes on in our soul between the attractions of the world that deluded us into thinking of this or that satisfaction as ultimate and the invitation to bind all that we are and do wholly to God. From this perspective, our being in the world and our service of others are not hindrances to spiritual progress but helps in disguise.

In the Third of these Dwelling Places, we sense in principle the paradoxical way in which God rewards his faithful servants. It is not be showering them with consolations but by asking them to endure for his sake a time of faith-testing. It will not disturb our deeper trust in God nor cause us to doubt the good will we have shown so far.

Amidst aridity, he may grant us for a relatively brief duration feelings of plentitude, tranquility, and peace. Accompanying these signs of grace may be the assurance that trials of faith mark the direction in which our life now has to go.

The tension associated with this stage of our journey is that God responds to our soul's longing at one and the same time with dryness and with a sense of plentitude. This flow from fullness to emptiness takes great trust to endure. In both cases, whether we feel cast down or lifted, we are sure that we can only find what we seek in God. To have tasted this plentitude and then to feel it being taken away makes us even more desirous of being wholly with our Beloved without interference from the vipers of worldliness who have no sense of our worth in God's eyes.

Saint John of the Cross articulates this classic struggle in *The Spiritual Canticle*. The bride-soul tastes and savors for a brief moment the presence of the Bridegroom. Then, alas, he goes away. The soul wants to chase after him with far more zeal than she has shown so far because she has now beheld the splendor of who he is. Theirs becomes a game of hide and seek. The Beloved gives her a glimpse of himself and then retreats, only to make her long for his presence with deeper ardor.

The tension portrayed in the Third Dwelling Places escalates because the soul desires God with her whole being. He responds to this longing with a few consolations complemented by many trials, all of which make the soul more humble. God seems to preserve her from the possible danger of becoming proud of her plentitude! It is as if he himself cannot risk that happening. Until the soul is sufficiently purified, he dare not outpour upon her more abundant graces. Without the trials she needs to make her fully faithful, she may not be ready to place her whole life in God's hands.

From the start of this search for self-knowledge to the light of truth at the center of the castle, the mystery accommodates itself to our need for mercy. Christ himself works within the parameters of our capacity to receive his grace. He waits upon us more than we wait for his coming. In his wisdom he wants us to turn in accordance with the pace of grace from stubborn resistance to total obedience, from selfish possessiveness to selfless charity. Once nothing stands between us and our Beloved, we are free to let our love be embodied in care and compassion for our neighbor. Having placed our self entirely in his hands, we grasp the plain truth that perfection consists not in consolations but in conformity to Christ and his cross. To be wholly abandoned is to accept with joy the invitations, challenges, and appeals he sends to us moment by moment. There is no other way to purify our pride-form than to trust in Christ's care for us despite the dryness we feel.

This plan of God has to be accompanied by great faith lest it arouse in us waves of frustration. We seemed to be making more progress than we had imagined. We felt the grace of inner plentitude. Now we wonder what God wants to tell us from one day to the next. We do what we can not to give in to these feelings of confusion and the irritation they may evoke. This sour disposition only exacerbates our sense of dissatisfaction with ourselves and God. These are the tricks of the Tempter. Though he knows he is not going to win this battle with ploys of prideful impatience, he displays his power by making us wonder why God simply does not do what he said he would. If coming to intimacy with him were a matter of doing good works, we would only be too happy to perform them. As Teresa reminds us: "…don't think He needs our works; He needs the determinations of our wills" (IC, 59:7).

These inner dialogues could mar the good that is being done in our soul were it not for the mystical pull of God offered to us in prayers of active recollection. Teresa distinguishes these from the prayer of quiet typical of the fourth mansions. Now the soul finds herself at a point of intentional meditation, which activates intellect, memory, and will. Later, in the phase of passive recollection, these three windows of the soul will come to rest in moments of simple union, which depend more on the state of our love-will than on our mind's questioning of what the will of God for us may be.

The prayer of active or receptive recollection opens the door to the castle a bit wider. Will we pass through it or step back once again? The favors we have already received convince us that we can converse with God on a friend-to-Friend basis. We "in-gather" or "collect ourselves" in receptivity to his initiative rather than making strenuous efforts on the part of our own will to make quicker progress. Needed most at this stage of our journey is a gentle orientation of our whole being to the Divine. This calm extension of longing love may last at first for only a few moments but soon it begins to permeate every day of our life like perfumed air. The good effects attributed to the penetration of our existence by the Divine Presence create around us an atmosphere of recollection that facilitates the movement from merely saying prayers to becoming living prayer. In turn our receptivity to the gift of infused contemplation increases.

On the ascetical level several threads intertwine. We learn from Teresa that out of dryness, we may "draw humility" (IC, 59:9) and that we must be fonder of the cross than of consolations. We understand that the trials happening to use are not caused by God but by our own deep-rooted disobedience. We do not yet comprehend all of the hidden chambers within us that God's grace has yet to purity. It is difficult for us to remain hopeful when we feel so desolate, but we must never despair. We would like to wash away the dark stains on our soul in an instant, but we are incapable of doing so. Compelled by the desire to become more purified, we may easily make the mistake of despairing our own faults and condemning those of others. We think we are responding to reality in humble manner until we see how proud we are of our humility! How we appraise these swirling thoughts—as endings or beginnings—will in many ways determine if we stop here or keep on following the lead of grace:

> I have known some souls and even many—I believe I can say—who have reached this state and have lived many years in this righteous and well ordered way both in body and soul, insofar as can be known. After these years, when it seems they have become lords of the world, at least clearly disillusioned in its regard, His Majesty will try them in some minor matters, and they will go about so disturbed and afflicted that it puzzles me and even makes me fearful. It's useless to give them advice, for since they have engaged so long in the practice of virtue they think that they can teach others and that they are more than justified in feeling disturbed (IC, 60:1).

Since perfectionism is itself a sin, it is of no help to our growth in humility. The habitual nature of such harmful temptations diminishes our freedom of spirit and makes us loathe to practice the moderate mortifications and penances required by our confessors. As we learn to let go of our own hunger for honor, we develop a healthier sense of discipline and discipleship. We find ourselves practicing more works of charity with less and less need to call attention to ourselves. We exercise more prudence in regard to our spiritual decorum in speech and dress, in the governing and organizing of what we have been tasked to oversee. In other words, our sense of intimacy with the Trinity begins to permeate all levels of our being. For example, in the vital dimension of our body, we do not go overboard in regard to excesses of fasting that may mar our health. Functionally, there is a sense of decorum in our relationships with others and in our business affairs. Spiritually, prayer is as natural to us as breath.

We see what is happening to us as a positive sign that we are on the way to being where God wants us to be in obedience to his will. We accept wholeheartedly that "doing our own will is usually what harms us" (IC, 65:12). We may derive several counsels at this point from a formative reading of the Third Dwelling Places. In summary, they are:

1. Don't let aridity perturb you. On the contrary, let it teach you the virtue of humility.

2. Render ready obedience to God's beckoning.

3. Look first at your own shortcomings and leave others alone.

4. Learn the art of respectful love. Live and let live. In short, "Take the log out of your own eye, and then you will see clearly to take the speck out of your neighbor's eye" (Matthew 7:15). Let us conclude these counsels with Teresa's own words:

> Let us look at our own faults and leave aside those of others, for it is very characteristic of persons with such well-ordered lives to be shocked by everything. Perhaps we could truly learn from the one who shocks us what is most important even though we may surpass him in external composure and our way of dealing with others. Although good, these latter things are not what is most important; nor is there any reason to desire that everyone follow at once our own path, or to set about teaching the way of the spirit to someone who perhaps doesn't know what such a thing is. For with these desires that God gives us, Sisters, about the good of souls, we can make many mistakes. So it is better to carry out what our rule says, to strive to live always in silence and hope, for the Lord will take care of these souls. If we ourselves are not negligent in beseeching His Majesty to do so, we shall, with His favor, do much good. May He be blessed forever (IC, 65-66:15).

Chapter 6
Entering Kingly Chambers

Consider Teresa's self-description of her state as a writer of the Fourth Dwelling Places. With complete integrity, she makes this candid admission:

> While writing this, I'm thinking about what's going on in my head with the great noise there that I mentioned in the beginning. It makes it almost impossible for me to write what I was ordered to. It seems as if there are in my head many rushing rivers and that these waters are hurtling downward, and that there are many little birds and whistling sounds, not in the ears but in the upper part of the head where, they say, the higher part of the soul is. And I was in that superior part for a long time for it seems this powerful movement of the spirit is a swift upward one. Please God I'll remember to mention the cause of this in discussing the dwelling places that come further on, for this is not a fitting place to do so, and I wouldn't be surprised if the Lord gave me this headache so that I could understand these things better. For all this turmoil in my head doesn't hinder prayer or what I am saying, but the soul is completely taken up in its quiet, love, desires, and clear knowledge (IC, 71:10).

The symptoms of chronic ailments to which Teresa confesses do not seem to interfere with experiences of mystical union in the core of her love life with the Lord. The tranquillity she desires and the clearness of mind for which she longs cannot be destroyed by any vital or functional failing. Souls who enter the fourth mansions find a peaceful flow of cooperation between their natural state and the supernatural status conferred on them by grace. Teresa testifies that many faithful souls attain this level of spirituality and benefit greatly from it. The subsequent stages of spiritual courtship, betrothal, and marriage reveal in those so chosen the reception of higher graces. God may reserve these gifts for fewer seekers since, accompanying their attainment, are more crosses to carry.

The degree of intensity of God's favor in these dwellings is interior detachment. Not only has the soul become progressively detached from worldly concerns as ultimate; she also begins to experience a letting go of the illusory contents of her own intellect, memory, and will. The understanding through faith the soul reaches, the remembrance of who she is that leaves her full of hope, the acts of love and charity she performs, point to her increasing reliance on God alone. She is less inclined to make any interior good—be it a thought, a memory, a desire—more important than its divine origin. Seeing its relative value enables her to bring her ideas in the present, her remembrances of the past, and her prayers for the future to greater realization. In her words, "the important thing is not to think much but to love much" (IC, 70:7).

A process of transformation now starts in earnest. As more acts of love are done, without her thinking about them or calculating their outcome, she begins to lead a life of inner simplicity and total trust in the Lord. God seemed to defer to her rhythms of openness to divine direction and to work within her capacity. Now the reverse is true: all that is in her rushes forward to follow God's lead and the pace of grace he sets for her. The Holy Spirit purges her understanding, illumines her memory, unites her will to his. This transformation occurs in such a courteous way that God's actions appear to be hers! "You are mine and I am yours," says the soul. This harmonious interconnection between her will and God's is like that between a conductor and a symphony orchestra. Her natural gifts and talents remain intact, but from this point onward, they intermingle with the supernatural..

As in all of the dwelling places, so in these there is a twofold approach to spiritual deepening. The mystical pull of God, the way of prayer practiced here, is passive recollection or the prayer of quiet. The soul "collects together" her faculties of intellect, memory, and will and enters into herself to be with God. This state of absorption in her innermost soul is unaffected by surface thoughts, imaginations, desires. Little bees may be buzzing in her head, but in her transfocal consciousness she experiences tranquillity and peaceful centering in God. Such is the chief characteristic of this state of prayer. Previously, the soul sought to find God "out there." Now she experiences an inward attraction moving from the center of her soul, where she is absorbed in God, to the care of outward affairs. Previously, she may have prayed "up" to the heaven. Now neither images of up nor down apply. Neither horizontal nor vertical matters distract her from her presence to the Divine Presence in the core of her being.

A centripetal force begins to take over in distinction from the centrifugal one that prevailed earlier in her story. This supernatural action draws her toward the deepest chambers in the castle. It does not depend on anything exterior to which the senses can bind themselves. All depends on the interior action of intimacy between the soul and God. The soul enters within her own center in Christ. It is difficult to put what happens into words, but the saint tries: "It seems that without any contrivance the edifice is being built, by means of this recollection, for the prayer that was mentioned. The senses and exterior things seem to be losing their hold because the soul is recovering what it had lost" (IC, 77:1). As she notes, this turn inward often happens to souls who are by nature inclined to enjoy the solitude that accompanies this movement. Already early in the spiritual life, they feel more at home with the prayer of quiet than with active recollection or discursive meditation.

Teresa's cautions in this regard echo those offered by Saint John of the Cross. Neither would advise anyone to leap into the prayer of quiet before passing through these earlier stages. Without the grace of God's leading, the side benefits of simple union may be felt, but the end results are shallow. Despite a natural inclination for this way of prayer, one must not overlook the dangers associated with wanting to jump into it on one's own timetable by skipping the stages of vocal and mental prayer and active recollection. In general such a move would be unwise, although Teresa again emphasizes that some souls are more naturally oriented toward interior prayer than others. There are signs by which to discern if the movement into the prayer of quiet is truly of God or only another pushy incentive on our part. A few of these are as follows.

The soul absorbed in God quiets her thoughts and reasoning powers. She maintains deep inner silence, keeping herself in readiness to receive any sign of the divine initiative. She disregards any personal advantage or gain she may derive from this experience. Her response is not to think much but to love much.

The prayer of quiet may coincide with certain spiritual feelings. Teresa feels it is imperative for us to understand the difference between infused "delights" and felt "consolations." This way of prayer may bestow on its recipients certain consoling sensations, but these differ from true interior delights felt in the presence of the Lord, thanks to the gift of his own peace. He takes our understanding, memory, and will and fixes them on him. Although these distinctively human faculties are not as yet fully aligned with his loving ways—as will happen in the state of union described by her as spiritual marriage—they are calm, quiet, and absorbed in God. In the saint's experience, there is a difference between being in union and being absorbed. She also confirms that the body itself may reverberate with this mystery as in the ecstatic state of being drawn above itself, above its suffering and situatedness. The delight that comes to her has to do with her being caught up in a magnitude of supernatural peace and joy. Any or all of these experiences may occur in the prayer of quiet. The difference is that consolations (*contentos*) have their source in our own nature and end in God: they are not infused. Spiritual delights (*gustos*) have their source in God and end in the prayer of infused recollection. We experience them in a natural way and we enjoy them as much, if not more, than any passing consolation.

Teresa returns to this distinction to make sure we understand that the sweetness of consolations proceeds from our own state of preparedness. It is that for which we long and may even labor to attain. Being consoled by God is good, provided we do not equate the spiritual life with the felt sensation of affective presence. What proceeds from our own nature is the need to feel some sign of God's love whereas spiritual delights in the proper sense proceed directly from God. They are granted by his initiative; they do not proceed from our own efforts or desires. The source of this inner stirring is his love whereas the source of lingering sweetness is our own nature. Both delights and consolations are experienced in a natural or bodily way. Both have about them an uplifting quality, but the difference comes from their source and our response to the divine agency.

Other distinctions follow in Teresa's teaching. Meditation may produce spiritual consolations whereas genuine delights occur more often in the prayer of quiet. Teresa compares sweetness to the basins that hold water attained from conduits a long way off. Consolation is like the basin that we bring to the spring. The sweetness that we feel may or many not enlarge our heart. If we strive too much for it, it can become an obstacle to the spiritual life. Spiritual delights always enlarge our inmost core, drawing our heart to intimacy with Divine Persons of the Trinity. Spiritual sweetnessess may prove to be obstacles to further intimacy if we start to focus on them. Delight in God always draws us toward intimacy because it begins and ends in him.

With the firmness characteristic of a great spiritual master, Teresa gives five reasons why we should not strive for consolations:

1. The first entails the fact that we should love God without any motive of self-interest.

2. The second is that we have to let God be God. We are not in charge of the progress of our own spiritual life.

3. The third is to be sure that our preparation for receiving these gifts includes a willingness to suffer with Christ and to imitate his lifestyle of appreciative abandonment to the mystery, whether or not we receive any consolations. After all, it is we who have offended him. Teresa insists that our embrace of Christ crucified comprises the truest preparation for a mature spiritual life. If God wills, we are to follow not the smoothest path, but the most difficult.

4. The fourth is because His Majesty is not obliged to grant these favors to us. His promise is that we may share in the glory of his reign on earth if we keep his commandments (cf. John 14:15). Teresa invites us to follow the way of love solely to serve our Lord, not to ask for consolations nor to desire them. We are to beg our Beloved not to give us these gifts in this life if they would deter us from our willingness to help him to carry his cross. Those who follow him in all sincerity can attest to this truth.

5. The fifth is a reminder that we should never feel as if we are laboring in vain. This water does not flow through conduits, as the other stream does, and so we gain nothing by fatiguing ourselves, however much we may practice meditation or, for that matter, subject

ourselves to excessive mortification. No matter how many tears we shed, we cannot produce water in any of these ways. Spiritual delights are given only to those whom God wills to receive them, often when one is not thinking about them at all. What Teresa concludes is that there is no point in our seeking in a push manner for any result since that would be a waste of energy. As long as *we* are at the center of our prayer life, what we derive from it, is *self*, not God. It is his prerogative to give consolations or delights to whomever he chooses and whenever he pleases.

These five points guide our journey in prayer past the turmoil of distracted thoughts and restless imaginations. The soul has to go much farther into the castle before she can be safe from the dangers posed by a life of wishful thinking, including her own laborious introspections and secret hopes for felt consolations. These movements tell the soul at this stage where she is not, while encouraging her not to forget where she is. She has moved progressively inside that place where lovers meet, thanks to the grace of God. She sees the difference between the work of a weak imagination and the flare-ups of devilish temptations. She does not blame herself anymore for what is clearly the devil's work. On the positive side she gains continually in self-knowledge. She experiences deep infused delights, all the while knowing that she has to let go of these divine touches, lest even they stand between her and God.

Some of the trials and interior struggles she knew in the second and the third mansions continue to plague her here, but she endures them in a more relaxed way, seeing all that happens to her as somehow part of God's ongoing plan for the soul's emergence in Christ. In the fifth, sixth and seventh mansions, she will enter the phases of spiritual courtship, betrothal, and marriage, but without passing through these preliminary stages no such openings can occur. Teresa tells us that she can say no more of these matters here but must move on to the next set of dwelling places. What she has described in the fourth mansions is "the one that more souls enter." In it "since the natural and the supernatural are joined," "the devil can do more harm" whereas in the places still to come "the Lord doesn't give him so much leeway" (IC, 84:13).

Chapter 7
Favors Granted to God's Special Guest

The Fifth Dwelling Places draw us into the wonders of spiritual courtship, forecasting the deepest intimacy of union with God: the oneness of our will with his. At the beginning of this section, Teresa pauses for prayer, and so must we, in preparation for the awesome mansions that are soon to unfold: "So, my Sisters, since in some way we can enjoy heaven on earth, be brave in begging the Lord to give us His grace in such a way that nothing will be lacking through our own fault; that He show us the way and strengthen the soul that it may dig until it finds this hidden treasure" (IC, 86:2).

What Teresa would like to consider, if the Lord is so good as to allow her to do so, is a description of this treasure as well as of the state of her own soul. As she begins to compose the Fifth Dwelling Places, she knows that her sisters are anxious to learn where this "little dove" is and how she plans to locate her nest. She cannot rest in spiritual consolations or earthly pleasures. She is destined to fly much higher than she has gone so far, but what will be asked of her in these last dwelling places?

Teresa acknowledges her lack of clarity in this regard. She begs God to help her to remember where she is in her narration since she has not found an opportunity to write for several months. Moreover, her head is not in a fit state to read through what she already composed. She apologizes for any confusion on her part. It is quite possible that she has repeated herself, but for her sisters such reiteration of wisdom is of no consequence. When one has been asked to write a masterpiece about the culminating stages of conformity to Christ, every word is precious.

The special favor granted by the grace of spiritual courtship is perseverance in interior detachment. Just as God grants the soul the wisdom of exterior detachment, so here he adds its inner extension. To let go of outer superfluity is a first step; to persevere in relinquishment and the inmost yielding of one's will to him is far more difficult. *To gain this virtue is to hold on to nothing but God and to everything in God.*

The soul reaches in this mansion and in those that follow the grace of self-abandonment to Divine Providence. She advances toward the stages of sanctity that lead to union with God. There are two types of oneness that Teresa identifies as passageways to consummation. Though courtship moves her along this holy path and espousal brings her to an intimacy with God that almost defies description, still greater ascetical and mystical graces await her if God deigns that she enter into the deeper chambers of the interior castle.

In Chapters One and Two, Teresa reemphasizes that mystical union is first and foremost a free gift. It is like delectable nourishment for hungry souls on the way to God. Even our outer nature may benefit from the depth of sacred awe that encompasses all that is. Quieted are the interior powers of thinking, remembering, anticipating. In silence the soul is readied by grace for this loving encounter with Christ. Grace alone carries her into this new way of life. In Chapters Three and Four, Teresa describes the glory of ascetical conformity to the cross by pointing retrospectively to the good that has happened to the soul, who persevered through the second, third, and fourth mansions. What she says of mystical union at this point forecasts what lies ahead in the Sixth and Seventh Dwelling Places as the soul enters the states of spiritual and espousal marriage.

Ascetical disciplines have become like a secondary tissue of dispositions in the life of the bride-soul. So refined is her response to grace that she is almost incapable of disobedience. Nonetheless it remains difficult for her nature to be at home with the additional mystical favors she receives. Despite moments of inner calm and tranquility, there are also times of tension between her outward appearances and perceptions and the gifts of contemplative union inundating her core form. Rather than trying to force a false peace, she reaffirms her determination not to follow her own plans but God's. Any suffering she experiences prepares her for more intimate encounters with the bridegroom of her soul. He beseeches her to come and rest in him now that she lives for love. Felt union may still be forthcoming, but faith union in love, even in the midst of aridity, is already hers. Suffering only serves to polish the diamond her soul has become. It offers her the privilege of entering into the Paschal Mystery and of comprehending the deepest meaning of the dying and rising of Christ. The high mystical graces that accompany spiritual marriage are forthcoming. The prayer of simple union, characteristic of this Dwelling Place, is a more refined expression of the prayer of quiet. Of it Teresa says:

> Don't think this union is some kind of dreamy state like the one I mentioned before. I say "dreamy state" because it seems that the soul is as though asleep; yet neither does it really think it is asleep nor does it feel awake. There is no need here to use any technique to suspend the mind since all the faculties are asleep in this state—and truly asleep—to the things of the world and to ourselves. As a matter of fact, during the time that the union lasts the soul is left as though without its senses, for it has no power to think even if it wants to. In loving, if it does love, it doesn't understand how or what it is it loves or what it would want. In sum, it is like one who in every respect has died to the world so as to live more completely in God (IC, 86:3).

What she means is that this advancement puts her soul fast asleep to the powers, pleasures, and possessions of this world, so completely has God overtaken her will. So intense is his love for her that she has no power to think beyond the liberating *yes* of obedience. There is nothing left of her own ego to interfere with this encounter. Its duration may be brief but intense; it is beyond any sense of temporal timing. When it comes to the spiritual life, this experience has no parallel. She says that the meeting between her and her Beloved always feels short and seems even shorter than it really is. Following this swift but sanctifying encounter, the soul is somewhat anxious because the consolations associated with these mystical graces disappear even faster than when they originally appeared, so much so that the saint has to admit that the soul is doubtful as to what really happened. Teresa repeats her concern because of the unusual events taking place in the interior life of the soul:

> I said that this union was not some kind of dreamy state, because even if the experience in the dwelling place that was mentioned is abundant the soul remains doubtful that it was union. It doubts whether it imagined the experience; whether it was asleep; whether the experience was given by God; or whether the devil transformed himself into an angel of light. It is left with a thousand suspicions. That it has them is good, for, as I have said, even our own nature can sometimes deceive us in that dwelling place (IC, 87:4).

These doubts may later fade in significance, but not until she has had a good deal of experience with this type of prayer. Now she wonders if such experiences might only be products of her imagination. Was she asleep? Was the favor she received a gift of God or was the devil transformed into an angel of light? She is tortured by a thousand suspicions. In spite of this obscurity and anxiety, the certitude she also feels cannot be shaken. Such is the paradox she has to endure: doubt on the one hand, conviction on the other. God implants himself in the center of her soul in such a way that when she returns to herself she is positive that their co-presence is fact, not fantasy.

In this set of rooms Teresa says, the soul is granted the grace of a first meeting with her future spouse. He comes to greet her in such a way that she can not "doubt that [she] was in God and God was in [her]. This truth remains with [her] so firmly that even though years go by without God's granting that favor again, the soul can neither forget nor doubt that [she] was in God and God was in [her]" (IC, 89:8).

This truth lasts a lifetime whether or not God ever grants her such a favor again. She can neither forget it nor be tempted to report that she never received it. The intensity of this experience reminds us that these Dwelling Places are not like steps on a ladder where one rung leads to the other. The grace of union can be given at one point in a person's life and then not recur for many years hence. The soul still recalls this wonder and feels inspired and edified by it.

From an ascetical perspective, the more God communicates himself to the soul, the more she longs for him, despite her acute awareness of the pitfalls and dangers she may have to endure. The slightest failure on her part to be loyal to him can throw her into despair. Will she have the courage to consent if God beckons her to go further into this unknown land? What is the degree of risk she has to take to submit to divine transformation? How will she handle the pain of her Beloved's apparent absence? No wonder she identifies with the torment of Christ when he said almost with his last breath, "My God, my God, why have you forsaken me?" (Matthew 27:46).

Is there a positive side to the harsh reality of God's nearness and distance during this courtship period? Being loved by God as much as she is enables the soul to forget herself and to rearticulate from the depth of her being her love for both God and neighbor. She culti- vates the docility typical of discipleship. She asks humbly to be led. Vulnerable though she feels due to sin, she knows in her heart how worthwhile in God's eyes she really is. He loves her unconditionally. Being detached from anyone or anything less than His Majesty has never been easier. Nothing that happens can deal a mortal blow to her now. No power in heaven or earth can imperil her soul. To gain God is to gain all she will ever need or desire. Pleasing God is her great- est delight, along with prayer and contemplation. Having died to the world, she lives "completely in God" (IC, 86:3).

Zeal for the good is another virtue she acquires. It is intolerable to her to offend her neighbor. She would sooner die than be a source of suffering for others. We learn from Saint Teresa that the highest mystical graces granted to us inwardly project us outward into works of charity. There is nothing in the fifth mansions that would lead us to cultivate a Jesus-and-I piety. Rather our lives become as other-oriented as his was.

From here onward, the soul's journey could be characterized in two main ways. First, her whole spiritual life from start to finish centers on encounters with the living God. His word to her is: "Strive always to advance." Second, she is like a hawk in her ability to spot the roving prey of sin. Her struggles with the Devil are fierce, but the victory belongs to the Lord. The Evil One has no power to interfere with the sweet grace of spiritual courtship granted to her, although he can inflict some turmoil within:

> It seems to me that the prayer of union does not yet reach the stage of spiritual betrothal. Here below when two people are to be engaged, there is discussion about whether they are alike, whether they love each other, and whether they might meet together so as to become

more satisfied with each other. So, too, in the case of this union with God, the agreement has been made, and this soul is well informed about the goodness of her Spouse and determined to do His will in everything and in as many ways as she sees might make him happy (IC, 103:4).

Theirs may have been but "one single short meeting," but it is powerful enough to reorient and transform her entire existence.

The main allegory Teresa uses to describe this transformation is that of the silkworm. This symbol offers a vivid and accurate description of the journey of the soul from the cocoon stage through that of metamorphosis to the emergence of the butterfly. The silkworm in the first stages of transformation draws energy from the heat which comes from the Holy Spirit. She relies on the grace God gives to all sincere seekers. Personal prayer and the reception of Holy Communion protect her like the cocoon builds a shield around the life within to make sure metamorphosis will occur and that the butterfly will emerge.

The soul then seeks to nourish herself with more heavenly food. Like the silkworm, she dwelt in a place where she died a death that marked the onset of her rebirth. The cocoon is understood here to mean Christ. The silkworm, which was once large and ugly, comes out of the cocoon as a beautiful butterfly. Now, thanks to the action of her Beloved, she can fly away from the safety of the cocoon and not be lost. The temptation to stay there is understandable. Christ's own apostles wanted to build tents and remain on Mount Tabor, but the Lord had other plans for them (cf. Matthew 17:1-8). Similarly the butterfly cannot escape the implications of her release. The soul, too, has to change. Despite all she has gained, she detects a few remnants of not being fully resigned to the will of God. Knowing that she must act in conformity to him as much as she can makes her resistance all the more regrettable. With many tears and much sorrow, she begs for forgiveness. She feels the tension of this trial since she is unable to do more than she has been given the grace to grow.

The soul, in short, is in a state of suspension. She has been set free. She has been transformed by love. She cannot return to her previous state, but she does not know how to proceed. Neither can she deny a continual urging from within to move toward betrothal and then on to spiritual marriage. Having already enjoyed profound intimacy with the Trinity, she wonders how her further longing for union can be realized?

From the fifth mansions emerge simple counsels chiseled on our heart like "Thy will be done." Many virtues come to fruition, especially humility or walking in truth of who we are. Another is detachment from anything or anyone that overly preoccupies us so that we can become like clear panes of glass through which rays of divine light shine. Mutual love can also be exercised in many ways, ranging from almsgiving to friendly words of encouragement when someone feels low. What God chooses to do with our corporal and spiritual works of mercy is not our concern; what counts is that we turn from self to others in generous, Christ-like compassion and care.

In this way we more and more resemble the Good Shepherd we love. This taste of union is different from the experience of "in-being" one might attain in certain esoteric practices at the end of which one often meets not the Divine Other but simply oneself. The "in-being" experience, if absolutized, can produce subtle effects of self-salvation. That is why a "counter" experience is so essential on the way of union. At every step of her movement into the castle's depths, the soul reaches out to the otherness of God for help and salvation. She knows she is in need of redemption. None of her "in-being" experiences like rapture, ecstasy, or elevation of consciousness are worth anything to her without the "counter" movement of her being grasped by God. The image of the Crucified Christ and meditation on his passion is highly recommended by Teresa, even in these last mansions. Without this sense of his otherness, of his being the only begotten Son of the Father, the Second Person of the Blessed Trinity, we might be tempted to lose awe, take God for granted, and rest in the cozy corners of our own good feelings.

Teresa sees the "in-being" of intimacy and the "counter-being" of surrender to Christ for the sake of serving others as mutually complementary. Both movements interform in a full religious experience. The enraptured side of presence to the Three Divine Persons comes together with the challenging companionship of the Incarnate Word. Emmanuel (God-with-us) renames us adopted children of the family of the Trinity with whom he wants to share the epiphanic light of eternal love during our earthly sojourn.

One feels in Teresa's words a brilliant capacity for checks and balances. Hers is not just a record of subjectivistic experiences. The saving presence of Christ, brought to light in the ecclesial doctrines she espouses, becomes a trustworthy foundation on which to pursue the purgative, illuminative, and unitive paths to formation, reformation, and transformation. We recall in Teresa's description of the "four waters" in *The Book of Her Life* that she relates the first water to the purgative way. Drawn from the well, it is comparable to vocal and mental prayer or meditation. The second water, which comes to us by means of a pulley system, can be compared to the prayer of quiet or the illuminative way. Both Teresa and John of the Cross hold that average Christians of good will and humble intention can advance to this stage of prayer. Its degree of grace is more readily available since many sincerely seeking souls may experience the art and discipline of active contemplation. The third water is like "liquid gold." It flows into the garden via a stream and is comparable to infused or passive contemplation. The best way to find the water is the fourth since rain provides it; it is related to the unitive way or the prayer of union and may be accompanied by true delights.

Teresa continues these descriptions of the life of prayer in the Fifth Dwelling Places. The first, second and the third mansions belong in great measure to the purgative way; they express the innate asceticism of our poverty of spirit, although mystical graces are granted each step of the way. The First Dwelling Places focus on vocal prayer, meditative reflection, and the state of friendship between the soul and God, which in itself represents a higher degree of intensity of grace. The Second Dwelling Places focus on mental prayer or meditation, often called the active life of friendship; it is the beginning of the spiritual life in a more recognizable sense. The Third Dwelling Places focus on simplified mental prayer, active recollection, and mature friendship, in short, on a disciplined and delightful spiritual life. Here one becomes more attentive to the need to reorient one's life in the direction of Gospel truths and to allow ample time and space for religious devotions like adoration of the cross. One seeks means of grace to nourish the life of the Spirit and to conform one's whole heart to Christ.

God never ceases working for our good and inspiring us to grow more closely to him. In response to the invitation of grace in the fourth mansions, Teresa describes the beginning of infused contemplation with its testing times of aridity together with the prayer of quiet or passive recollection. These experiences are felt in more or less degrees of intensity, but all of them, are all modes of falling in love with God by means of the blessed encounters he initiates in our soul.

These touches, invitations, and appeals, whose agony comes from on high, make it impossible for such a seeker to be in any way preoccupied with herself. Her only activity is to pay attention to the graces God sends her. She does what she can not to let them go by or be forgetful of them. As these meetings between her and God become the centerpiece of her existence, she advances to the threshold of the experiences described by Saint John of the Cross in *The Ascent of Mount Carmel* as the active nights of sense and spirit.

The unitive way, reserved by Teresa for the Fifth, Sixth, and Seventh Dwelling Places, reveals special degrees of intensity of grace, more related to the passive nights of sense and spirit in which the soul is wholly receptive to the divine initiative. She enters into the prayer of simple union on the way to the prayer of full union characterized by bridal mysticism with its stages of courtship, betrothal, and marriage. Together these phases of Christian maturity mark the culmination of the transformation process begun when the soul first entered the castle.

Each degree of grace leads her soul further into the heart of pure love. Soul, psyche, and spirit enjoy the fruits of intimacy: companionship and lifelong fidelity to the Lord. Her "I" now becomes the "I" of Christ living in her. This grace of participative transformation is that toward which the soul has gravitated from mansion to mansion. The movement she undergoes is at once inward and upward, linear and circular. In the sixth and seventh mansions, there is a reiteration of the virtues that are part of this state of friendship, only now they are lived with increasing intensity. There is a heightened awareness of having been granted a person-to-Person relationship with God. His agenda for progress unfolds not by force but by tender accommodation to the true self that she is and was meant to be.

God works in a unique way in each soul he creates. There are common graces and experiences all share, but, just as in the field of medicine so in soul-therapy, each treatment is designed to help each person uniquely. God respects that about us which escapes reduction to a nameless collectivity. We show our gratitude to him by respect-

ing the communal side of our call, but such shared knowledge has
to be filtered through the windows of our uniqueness. Teresa herself
expresses profound respect for the gifts she has been given by God
while deferring to the needs of each of her sisters. This passage from
the end of the Fifth Dwelling Places is noteworthy in this regard:

> May he be pleased that I manage to explain something
> about these very difficult things. I know well that this
> will be impossible if His Majesty and the Holy Spirit
> do not move my pen. And if what I say will not be for
> your benefit, I beg Him that I may not succeed in say-
> ing anything. His Majesty knows that I have no other
> desire, insofar as I can understand myself, but that His
> name be praised and that we strive to serve a Lord who
> ever here on earth pays like this. Through His favors
> we can understand something of what He will give us
> in heaven without the intervals, trials, and dangers that
> there are in this tempestuous sea. If there were no dan-
> ger of losing or offending Him, it would be easy to
> endure life until the end of the world so as to labor for
> so great a God and Lord and Spouse.
>
> May it please His Majesty that we may merit to render
> Him some service, with0out as many faults as we al-
> ways have, even in good works, amen (IC, 106:11).

Chapter 8
Rooms Almost Too Exquisite to Describe

Prior to embarking on the difficult descriptions of spiritual betrothal in the Sixth Dwelling Places, Teresa interjects some information about herself with which all of us can relate:

> I am struggling, Sisters, to explain for you this action of love, and I don't know how. For it seems a contradiction that the Beloved would give the soul clear understanding that He is with it and yet make it think that He is calling it by a sign so certain that no room is left for doubt and a whisper so penetrating that the soul cannot help but hear it. For it seems that when the Spouse, who is in the Seventh Dwelling place, communicates in this matter (for the words are not spoken), all the people in the other dwelling places keep still; neither the senses, nor the imagination, nor the faculties stir. O my powerful God, how sublime are your secrets, and how different spiritual things are from all that is visible and understandable here below. There is nothing that serves to explain this favor, even though the favor is a very small one when compared with the very great ones you work in souls (IC, 116:3).

Teresa confesses that she feels at a loss for words to describe sublime experiences that escape the limits of articulation. In her humility she is aware that whatever she manages to say contains much more that she is capable of expressing. She makes us aware without regret that not all souls are led along the path of espousal whereas everyone can come to intimacy with the Divine according to the degree of love God allows them to experience. In her autobiography, *The Story of a Soul,* Saint Thérèse of Lisieux asked her sister Pauline to explain the mystery of God's grace to her. Rather than lecture the child, she tells her to fetch a thimble from the sewing room and a tumbler from the kitchen. Then she directs Thérèse to fill each vessel to the rim with water after which she must answer a single question: "Which of the two are the fullest?" Thérèse responds correctly that both are filled to their capacity. And so, replies her wise sister, it is the same with God's grace. His Majesty fills each of us to the fullest capacity with the grace he intends to grant. Our spiritual life may lead us to "thimblehood" or "tumblerhood," depending on which vessel we happen to be. God will not withhold any of the grace meant to fill our thimble or our tumbler. He loves us to the fullness of our capacity to receive his love in accordance with his divine plan for our lives. Perhaps it is safe to say that the high mystical stages described here can be compared to "tumblerhood."

Teresa cautions that anyone who arrives at these stages in the spiritual life might herself become the victim of another's envy. This occurrence causes the soul to suffer a great deal, but so does its opposite. Instead of being envied, she becomes the recipient of excessive praise. This attention causes her to feel even more terrible. She knows that whatever happens to her does not come from her own power but from God. Teresa describes how much she dislikes praise and the sufferings it caused her to go through at this stage. The special favor of God granted to her soul in this mansion is total surrender. Her response has to be one of patient endurance. She has to let God work with her at his pace in his own good time. She, who has been wounded by love for her Spouse, seeks every opportunity to be out of the public eye. She would like to renounce all that disturbs her solitude, knowing that "...no consolation is allowed in the midst of this tempest" (IC, 112:9). There is no remedy for it "but to wait for the mercy of God" (IC, 113:10).

Required of her at this time of abandonment to Divine Providence is complete openness to God's initiative. The only action possible on her part is patience. Such waiting is not easy once one has been wounded by love. There is no place left for her to hide. She has to absorb these woundings in silent surrender, especially when they draw attention to herself or occur in the midst of daily tasks. Life has to go on as normally as possible despite the tidal waves of divine desire that draw her more deeply into God. Experiences of blame and praise are equally problematic. Rightly or wrongly, she does not respond to either with defensiveness. So banished is her false self that all that is left in her heart are the virtues of love and forgiveness. Though she may, in the case of blame, be unjustly accused, misunderstood, or ridiculed, she will not respond with excuses or try to make herself look good. She will see this event as another opportunity to receive a wound of love, sent by her Beloved to test the truth of her promises. The same goes for praise. Not only does she feel embarrassed by it, knowing how unworthy she is to receive these graces; she also sees it as another instance of God's wounding her by making her feel more humble and unworthy of the compliments she receives.

At this time God may allow infirmity to grip her on the vital level like the buzzing noises Teresa reports raging in her head. For her this physical incapacity, too, is translated into a wound of love in which she finds a message of how God works through her physical weakness. In other words, she is able to see each of these situations as openings to be united more deeply with his love-will for her. He offers her what she can bear and no more than that. He does not test her or anyone beyond their strength to endure.

Another torture she describes concerns an encounter she had with a scrupulous and inexperienced confessor (cf. IC, 111:8-9). She sees this painful event as a grace received especially in her situation as a woman religious. Instead of complaining about it, she tries to translate it into another way in which God wounds her for her own good. This interpretation, far from weakening her resolve, empowers her to seek a new confessor. Once more she uses this event as a formation opportunity allowed by God for her own and others' sanctification.

What Teresa manifests so well are the dispositions of heart, mind, and will she must retain in all costs and in all circumstances. She trains herself to see these events as openings to her becoming more aware of God's work in her life, of how he shows his special love for souls in the here-and-now situation they must shepherd. Teresa's attitude is that the Father loves her enough to allow her to bear many burdens as his Son did. The effect this surrender has on her is to enhance her peace and patience in the face of whatever God may ask of her in the wisdom of his Providence. The depth of this commitment prevails despite any ferment stirring the surface of her life. Though there are severe distresses to be found in her present circumstances, interiorly, in the core of her being, she experiences the calming quietude of resting in God as the ground of charitable activity. By translating all of these experiences into instances of God's both wooing and wounding her for love's sake, she is able to walk the way of the cross with joy.

Here we find another indelible link between the ascetical and the mystical life and the soul's cooperation with both kinds of graces. An intimate dialogue goes on between Christ and the soul. He directs her attention to seeing in every obstacle a formation opportunity. He fills her heart with a fervent desire to identify with his death and resurrection. Her wholly surrendered response can only be attributed to Christ himself as the source of every inspiration. Such instances of transforming love cannot be attributed to any devilish trick. So much good happens to her amidst these trials that she breathes a sigh of relief. Gains and pains, joys and sorrows are signals of the Lord's beckoning her to deeper intimacy.

On the side of the mystical infusion of graces, she is taken, so to speak, out of herself and into the embrace of the Divine Persons. This outward and upward flow happens quite literally in such experiences as ecstasy, rapture, flight of the spirit, and the arrow of fire. These images represent Teresa's attempts to describe what the soul goes through at heightened moments of mystical intensity, but such uplifts to heavenly places are ultimately beyond human descriptions. In all of these experiences the soul undergoes as well a certain degree of suffering. It is as nothing compared to the exquisite delight that the living flame of love installs by tenderly wounding her in her deepest center. The purpose of these graces is not to flatter her or to make her feel special, but to conform her spirit to the living God.

Moving with these graces and the waters flowing from the previous Dwelling Places, the soul reaches a new threshold of transformation. God has purged her intellect of the necessity to comprehend in an analytical fashion what is happening to her. She is free to enter into the realm of mystery. In the Fifth Dwelling Places grace took her will, detached her from any created thing as ultimate, and attached her to the Divine Will. Now she is able to return to ordinary life in a non-possessive fashion. In the Sixth Dwelling Places, grace tempers the sensitivity that fraught her soul. She registers with equal love and forgetfulness her feelings of consolation and desolation. Of central importance is her desire to surrender entirely to God. She allows her intellect, memory and will, her affection and anticipation to be attuned to Christ's presence, to his call. She stands on the threshold of full submission of her interior powers to His Majesty. She intuits all that she undergoes for love's sake as no longer under the control of her will. The preparatory dispositions of yielding to God, already granted to her in the earlier mansions, now come to culmination. The struggles of her soul to live in faith, hope, and love, in humility, detachment, and charity, now seem of little consequence compared to the exquisite experience of interior transformation described in the Sixth Dwelling Places. The Lord is close enough to her now to fight off the rest of her foes. She does not have to face or fear them anymore:

> For at an unexpected time, with one word alone or a chance happening, He so quickly calms the storm that it seems there had not been even as much as a cloud in that soul, and it remains filled with sunlight and much more consolation. And like one who has escaped from a dangerous battle and been victorious, it comes out praising our Lord; for it was He who fought for the victory. It knows very clearly that it did not fight, for all the weapons with which it could have defended itself are seen to be, it seems, in the hands of its enemies. Thus, it knows clearly its wretchedness and the very little we of ourselves can do if the Lord abandons us. (IC, 113:10)

This awareness of Christ's being with her at every moment and in every situation shields the soul from anxious feelings. Having come to the realization articulated by the early Father of the Church, Saint Ireneaus, that "the glory of God is the human person fully alive," Teresa is able to appreciate both her uniqueness and the common sense ways in which she has to live her conventual commitments. The fuller her experience of union is, the richer is her grasp of her unique-communal calling in Christ. Obedience does not erase her individuality; it allows for the true emergence of her personhood in Christ. Teresa of Avila is not a saint on a pedestal but a real person with whom we can identify.

The crux of this experience rests in her knowing the difference between her creaturehood and her Creator. This recognition of her finitude is not a cause for alarm but a key to her happiness. Her Christian religious consciousness goes hand in hand with the recognition of her creatureliness. Her having been made in the image and likeness of God (cf. Genesis 1:26-27) bestows upon her a dignity beyond any honor the world could bestow. It evokes in her soul an identification with the mystery of the Trinity and the Word Incarnate in whom she lives and moves and has her being (cf. Acts 17-28).

Several special experiences recorded in the sixth mansions stem from extraordinary graces that are not essential for contemplative living in daily acts of charity. These graces may or may not be granted to everyone. Such explicitations of God's way with us, as Teresa is careful to confirm, are not necessary for union. The danger of their playing upon our pride-form cannot be discounted. For this reason we need to relativize them and return to interior quiet, peacefully abiding with God in our soul. Teresa insists that we must never take delight in these mystical graces as ends in themselves. Neither must we be presumptuous about having received them. With such cautions in mind, she goes on to describe:

1. In Chapter 3:   Interior Words or Locutions

2. In Chapter 4:   Rapture, Ecstasy, Trance

3. In Chapter 5:   Flight of the Spirit

4. In Chapter 9:   Imaginary and Intellectual Visions

5. In Chapter 11: Arrow of fire

Interior Words or Locutions

These communications express messages that comfort and guide the soul at trying times during her life. She may hear, not so much audibly as with the ears of her heart, a scriptural phase like "Be not troubled, it is I, fear not." As soon as this interior word touches the substance of her soul, she experiences great peace. Teresa suggests three criteria by which to discern whether or not these locutions are to be trusted as coming from God rather than being mere products of our imagination:

1. Corporeal locutions heard in a recognizable, auditory way are most to be distrusted since they are vulnerable to exaggeration. One thinks of the proverbial "fish story" where the minnow hooked becomes a major catch!

2. Imaginary locutions heard in a less auditory way may seem to be more trustworthy, but they, too, need to be rather swiftly dismissed since they could be caused by other spirits seducing our tendency to vainglory.

3. Intellectual or spiritual locutions that resonate in the deepest core of our being are most likely to be discerned as coming from God. They are the most trustworthy sources of divine self-communication.

Corporeal locutions, as the phase itself suggests, stimulate our physical powers of hearing and can tempt us to call more attention to ourselves than to God. Imaginary locutions, precisely because they are apprehended by our fantasy-making faculty, present another set of problems. Even though they are heard with no outer ear involved, they originate in an area of our being that must be subjected to careful scrutiny, especially if we tend to have an active imagination anyway.

After the fact, in retrospect, it may seem to us as if something of value has been received like an impression of our finger on wax, but such happenings are still too corporeal for Teresa's comfort. She has most faith in intellectual locutions because God whispers what he has to say in the depths of her soul. She apprehends no voice that is either corporeal or imaginary, only an expression of certain confirmations of faith in the depths of her understanding, memory, and will. Some sure signs that these locutions are from God (cf. 120-121: 5-7) include the imprint they make on her interior life. It as silent as the gentle passing of a divine breeze (cf. 1 Kings 19:11) because God communicates to her in a pure way. These disclosures carry with them a sense of his power and authority, both in themselves and in the actions that emanate from them.

Teresa is sensitive to the necessity to incarnate what is being communicated to her inwardly. She desires to link this inner message with its external fruit in charitable decisions, dispositions, and actions. A familiar phrase like "Be not afraid," experienced deep within her soul, has the effect both inwardly and outwardly of calming her, of making her more attuned to the immediate needs of others and of her own inspired goals. Her troubles seem to be lifted from her. She feels wondrously comforted. She acquires new confidence. What she receives is not an esoteric bit of gnostic information but a text of incarnated wisdom in which Christ comforts her soul experientially. She swiftly acts upon the directives indicated by this gift and the residue of tranquility that lingers in her soul.

The actional component associated with intellectual locutions leaves her more ready than ever to sing God's praises and do his will. A word received from His Majesty is enough to motivate her to become his messenger with tireless courage and untarnished candor. The words she has been given do not vanish from her memory for a long time. Some never disappear at all. The texts that stay with Teresa like "Don't be distressed" represent words she knows Christ spoke to her intimately and directly. They left her with a conviction of complete certainty. Doubts may be raised by others, they may even invade her own mind, but she does not and cannot deviate from their veracity. She knows that the devil only puts these doubts into her head because he wants to distress her and to deter her from the work God wants her to do. Rather than pay any attention at all to such signs of uncertainty, she chooses to focus solely on Christ. In the end, this word of the Lord will be fulfilled with complete devotion and without any fear or doubt.

Teresa compares these powerful words to prophetic passages from the Old Testament. At the time they were uttered, people may have questioned their validity. The prophets themselves may have begged God to refrain from giving them the task of telling others what he told them. The proof of their truth lay in their divine fulfillment. Teresa identifies with such a commission. She knew the assurances she received from God were true because they were fulfilled in her life experientially. She grew less troubled and fearful. Her confidence that Christ would not leave her soared to greater heights. Had such locutions come from her imagination or from the devil, none of these signs would have accompanied them. These words themselves would have borne no such power and authority nor would she have been given the assurance that promises thus spoken would be pledges attained.

Further signs that these locutions are from God and not products of mere wish-fulfillment also merit analysis by Saint Teresa. Words emerging from these intellectual and spiritual depths are less distinct than the sounds we normally hear. They come to us as in a dream. They go beyond the capacity for human articulation. Their reception usually comes unexpectedly. More often than not, the soul has not been thinking about them at all. Neither has she asked for these disclosures. Imaginative locutions, to the contrary, can be tied to one's cogitating her thinking about them whereas true communications that are from God are suddenly there. Her mind was farthest away from them. She had no particular thoughts about these or any other self-communications of God to her. Keeping still about them was more the rule than the exception. She dreaded projecting anything from her own imagination onto God. Nor did she want anyone to think that she heard these words with her bodily ears.

When God is their source, it is as if Another gave them to her. The message may be the last one she thought she would hear, but it is the best one she could possibly receive. The difference between her self-talk and these divine communications is obvious. In imaginary locutions there seems to be a great many words with different connotations attached to them. In genuine locutions one word may contain a world of meaning that could not be put as clearly into one's understanding, no matter the amount of verbiage used. Much more is understood than the words themselves convey. There is a wealth of wisdom in one small phase. A surplus of unspoken meaning can be found in what has been heard with the inner ears of her heart.

Rapture, Ecstasy, Trance

In Chapter Four Teresa describes these extraordinary phenomena to the best of her ability, stressing for the sake of the doubters surrounding her that they are not attributable merely to a woman's weaknesses. The soul does feel drawn out "of her senses," which is the literal meaning of the word ecstasy. In the midst of them she is absorbed and suspended yet fully awake to the leading of the Spirit. Since she is incapable of grasping all that is happening to her, her most ardent desire is to bow to the agency of her Beloved. Gone is any capacity on her part to resist what God initiates when he draws her toward himself in such an explicit way. These moments thankfully last only for a relatively brief duration. The test of their veracity is that any willful prolonging of them spoils their giftedness. Experiences this unusual can occur as God allows, but in no way should one judge the quality of his or her spiritual life on the basis of them alone.

Flight of the Spirit

In Chapter Five Teresa depicts another mystically infused grace that closely resembles rapture, although it is experienced by the soul in a different, much faster way. It is as if the soul takes part in a rapid motion that transports her into another plane of consciousness. The flight of the spirit could be compared to what happens at the moment of death as when Saint John of the Cross says that we "break through the veil of this sweet encounter." The soul seems to have left her body yet she is taught so many things at once that she cannot possibly interpret or grasp them all. Lifted seemingly into the company of the saints, she receives an ecstatic affirmation of her soul's immortality and the blessed assurance that life goes on after death. No longer is she afraid of her mortality. She senses what it means to move out of her body into another state of being. This flight of the spirit leaves in her soul a residue of great courage, faith, and confidence. It ends with an increase of her already tremendous love of God and her appreciation of the life he has given her. Having had a direct experience of the finite being pierced by the Infinite, all that is, was, and will be becomes more precious to her. Though life passes swiftly away, she has every reason to be grateful.

Imaginary and Intellectual Visions

When Teresa discusses the veracity or lack thereof of visions, she offers the same distinctions posited in her consideration of locutions, namely corporeal, imaginary, and intellectual. One word of advice she gives is that the devil may interfere more frequently with bodily and imaginative visions than with those that are intellectual. It would not behoove her to dismiss entirely what imaginary experiences may yield. There is some good in what is impressed on her soul insofar as it may influence her for a while. In intellectual visions the depth dimension of their meaning is inexhaustible since they come directly from God. Imaginary visions are closer to the corporeal. They make us more prone to deception, but, under the impact of proper methods of discernment, they can move us closer to the intellectual or spiritual essence of God's self-communications. To the degree that visions veer toward the corporeal, the danger increases that they are and may continue to be more self-initiated than God-given. The more they engage the intellectual substance of our soul, the more likely it is that they have been initiated by God. Through them, he impresses on us a way of seeing that enables us to grasp the meaning of what may previously have been unclear to us.

The more intellectual these visions are, the less likely they are to be linked with purely imaginative ideas or desires. Teresa admits that to appraise the source of such experiences is not easy. One can be deceived by personal ambitions to look more spiritual in the eyes of others than one really is. The demonic slips quickly into such crevices of self-centeredness. That is why wise, learned, and experienced spiritual direction in such delicate matters is not a luxury but a necessity. The greatest protection the soul receives is to walk in the truth of who she is before God and others. Illusions and false claims to be a visionary are treacherous obstacles to humility. Conformity with her Spouse requires this one virtue above all others:

> Once I was pondering why our Lord was so fond of this virtue of humility, and this thought came to me—in my opinion not as a result of reflection but suddenly: It is because God is supreme Truth; and to be humble is to walk in truth, for it is a very deep truth that of ourselves we have nothing good but only misery and nothingness. Whoever does not understand this walks in falsehood. The more anyone understands it the more he pleases the supreme Truth because he is walking in truth. Please God, Sisters, we will be granted the favor never to leave this path of self-knowledge, amen (IC, 165:7).

Arrow of Fire

In the eleventh chapter of the sixth mansions, Teresa describes a wound of love so deep that it transcends any category of physical pain and sears like a brand the soul's inmost center. This fiery arrow passes through her as swiftly as a flash of lightening. For as long as it lasts the soul cannot think of anything concerning her own affairs nor for that matter is there any source of personal suffering comparable to it. The arrow penetrates her body in a purely mystical way. This extraordinary experience is peculiar to the makeup of the soul who receives it; it is in no way a necessity for the pursuit of a mature spiritual life. We admire Teresa's honesty in attempting to describe such an event since undiscerning people might accuse her of anything from a sexual fantasy to a fainting spell! In trying to describe the indescribable, Teresa says it felt like a "smoking fire that though painful can be endured" (IC, 166:2). At a certain moment in her life of prayer, God struck her in an extremely powerful way. It was as if his love pierced through her whole body, mind, and spirit, instantly transforming her in the depths of her being and drawing her indelibly closer to him. What took place was not a fantasy made up by a frustrated woman. To the contrary, love itself catapulted her beyond mere finite, limited, bodily experiences to an upward thrust of pure transcendence.

Teresa suffered from the intensity of the extraordinary. She felt embarrassed at having these events occur in private or in public. She also felt such feelings revealed a lack of humility. She had no choice but to cooperate with the graces and trials God sent. Her growing love for the daily mortifications and little dyings, present in all situations, marked the death of all forms of selfish egocentric love and the rebirth of her concentration on divine love and its transforming power. God in his utterly transcendent otherness drew her to himself in his immanent nearness. To offend him in any way would be the worst sin imaginable to her.

Toward the end of this mansion, Teresa offers several counsels to those whom God has guided to this stage of faith deepening. They might be articulated in several intertwining directives like:

1. Be courageous. It is necessary for souls on fire with the love of God to pass through many trials if they are to advance at his choosing to the next stage of spiritual marriage.

2. Praise and thank God for the knowledge these mystical graces bestow on sincerely seeking souls. No amount of abstract learning can be a substitute for concrete experience.

3. Remember that the best remedy for concern about your spiritual progress is to occupy yourself with contemplative substitutes for concrete experience.

4. Engage in meditation on the sacred humanity of Jesus lest you get caught in esoteric speculations that will only weaken your faith.

5. Choose a mystery from the life of Christ and let it be impressed upon your memory. Consider it with simple regard. Remember who he is, what he has done for you, and how lacking in gratitude you might have been. Let this meditation on his sacred humanity be your anchor, especially when you are inclined to soar off like a high-flying kite into thoughts and images that transcend what God wants you to do and endure at this time.

6. Despite your experience of being lifted beyond what is earthbound, return as quickly as possible to the humanity of the Lord and let him be your way into the family of the Trinity.

7. Do not let yourself be so lost in the wonder of Christ's divinity that you lose touch with the workaday world of his humanity.

Souls purified by suffering and espoused to God stand now on the threshold of the seventh mansions like faithful souls ready to enter heaven. This state of spiritual marriage is as close to living eternity on earth as one could hope to experience. Were such a blessing possible, it would be as if the soul were allowed by God to suffer her Purgatory during this life so that she can enter heaven the second she exhales her last breath. Teresa says of such souls that "in the very end, before they die, He will pay for everything at once" (IC, 171:12). No matter how diligently she tries to articulate these favors, no words are adequate to do so. She begs God for the light she needs to communicate in such a way that others may benefit from what she herself has seen and experienced. Her wish is that nothing will hinder the celebration of spiritual marriage God destines for our soul. As she writes at the start of the Seventh Dwelling Places:

> You will think, Sisters, that since so much has been said about this spiritual path it will be impossible for anything more to be said. Such a thought would be very foolish. Since the greatness of God is without limits, His works are too. Who will finish telling of His mercies and grandeurs? To do so is impossible, and thus do not be surprised at what was said, and will be said, because it is but a naught in comparison to what there is to tell of God. He grants us a great favor in having communicated these things to a person through whom we can know about them. Thus the more we know about His communication to creatures the more we will praise His grandeur and make the effort to have esteem for souls in which the Lord delights so much. Each one of us has a soul, but since we do not prize souls as is deserved by creatures made in the image of God we do not understand the deep secrets that lie in them. May it please His Majesty, if He may thereby be served, to move my pen and give me understanding of how I might say something about the many things to be said that God reveals to the one whom He places in this dwelling place. I have earnestly begged this of His Majesty

since He knows that my intention is to make known His mercies that His name may be more praised and glorified (IC, 172-173:1).

The challenge she faces in approaching this last mansion and trying to describe its wonders is almost more than she can bear. How could anyone dare, except under obedience, to put words on such awesome experiences as the prayer of perfect union, the bond of spiritual marriage, and the Trinitarian mystery, fleetingly revealed but forever concealed in the Seventh Dwelling Places.

Chapter 9
At the Center of the Soul

Saint Teresa exercises great candor in her depiction of the state of her soul prior to that moment of consuming union in which she meets her Beloved in a foretaste of the life to come. Much to her amazement in these seventh mansions, it is as if the Lord himself longs to abide her heart, as if it is a kind of second heaven for him. The degree of intensity of grace granted by God at this juncture of her journey is that of complete harmony. The highest degree of oneness with the Trinity that it is possible to attain in this life has now radically entered into and reformed her soul.

In the Sixth Dwelling Places she records the delight associated with the conscious awareness of how near she was to God. These touches of union came to her with favors that made her humble. Their intensity soon lessened, but their memory lingered on. In the state of union, she is no longer able to speak of the bestowal by God of a passing touch but of an all-consuming awareness of the indwelling presence of the Three Divine Persons. This prayer of perfect union is the complement of an intellectual Trinitarian vision that reverberates in the substance of her soul. It differs from an imaginary one in that there is no strict correlation between what she sees and what she actually experiences. The gratuity of this vision changes her life. Its efficacy cannot be denied. It has no direct causes attributed to her because it is wholly supernatural, a matter of pure grace. She sees, not with human eyes but with a kind of visionary "seeing into" or intimacy with Father, Son, and Holy Spirit. The doctrine of the Trinity ceases being for her merely a catechetical truth of her faith; it becomes a living reality:

> Our good God now desires to remove the scales from
> the soul's eyes and let it see and understand, although

in a strange way, something of the favor He grants it. When the soul is brought into that dwelling place, the Most Blessed Trinity, all three Persons, through an intellectual vision, is revealed to it through a certain representation of the truth. First there comes an enkindling in the spirit in the manner of a cloud of magnificent splendor; and these Persons are distinct, and through an admirable knowledge the soul understands as a most profound truth that all three Persons are one substance and one power and one knowledge and one God alone. It knows in such a way that what we hold by faith, it understands, we can say, through sight—although the sight is not with the bodily eyes nor the eyes of the soul, because we are not dealing with an imaginative vision. Here all three Persons communicate themselves to it, speak to it, and explain those words of the Lord in the Gospel: that He and the Father and the Holy Spirit will come to dwell with the soul that loves Him and keeps His commandments (IC, 175:6).

By a wonderful kind of knowledge given to her from on high, she realizes the Oneness of the Three. What she once accepted as a tenet of faith has been confirmed through inner sight. Having been drawn to the mystery of the Trinity from the time of her baptism was in itself a grace beyond deserving. How much greater it is that the faith conveyed by the Church has become God's word for her. This vision leads the solitary seeker that she is from the pain of loneliness to the joy of solitude in which she enjoys the companionship of the Trinity and through this union of her community and indeed all of creation.

This wondrous dance of intimacy culminates in the celebration of spiritual marriage between her and her Beloved. The union of her heart with the Heart of Christ is analogous to the blessing of marital intimacy itself. According to Teresa:

> In the spiritual marriage, there is still much less re-
> membrance of the body because this secret union
> takes place in the very interior center of the soul,
> which must be where God Himself is, and in my
> opinion there is no need of any door for Him to enter.
> I say there is no need of any door because everything
> that has been said up until now seems to take place by
> means of the senses and faculties, and this appearance
> of the humanity of the Lord must also. But that which
> comes to pass in the union of the spiritual marriage is
> very different. The Lord appears in this center of the
> soul, not in an imaginative vision but in an intellectual
> one, although more delicate than those mentioned, as
> He appeared to the apostles without entering through
> the door when He said to them *pax vobis*. What God
> communicates here to the soul in an instant is a se-
> cret so great and a favor so sublime—and the delight
> the soul experiences so extreme—that I don't know
> what to compare it to. I can say only that the Lord
> wishes to reveal for that moment, in a more sublime
> manner than through any spiritual vision or taste, the
> glory of heaven. One can say no more—insofar as
> can be understood—than that the soul, I mean the
> spirit, is made one with God. For since His Majesty
> is also spirit, He has wished to show His love for us
> by giving some persons understanding of the point to
> which this love reaches so that we might praise His
> grandeur. For He has desired to be so joined with the
> creature that, just as those who are married cannot be
> separated, He doesn't want to be separated from the
> soul (IC, 178:3).

In the Seventh Dwelling Places, we see the benevolent combination of an intellectual vision of the Trinity and a personal love relationship between the soul and the Divine Word. Again Teresa explains:

> In the spiritual marriage the union is like what we have when rain falls from the sky into a river or fount; all is water, for the rain that fell from heaven cannot be divided or separated from the water of the river. Or it is like what we have when a little stream enters the sea, there is no means of separating the two. Or, like the bright light entering a room through two different windows; although the streams of light are separate when entering the room, they become one (IC, 179:4).

Even at this high state of union, there is in this mansion a two-fold dynamic between the mystical favors being granted to the soul as expressions of divine grace and the ongoing necessity of ascetical preparation. The discipline that undergirds this highest state of union refers to the attainment of a kind of ethical perfection or inner ordering of one's life according to the situation providentially designed by God for the soul's good. It entails a deep listening to Christ's Word in her heart and a willingness to be an instrument he can use to inspire others to become more like him. The interior union of bridal mysticism flows into the mundane corners of everyday life. There is in the soul a heightened sense of what Christ has had to do to turn her life around and to free her from the sins and deceptions that masked the penetration of her soul by the Divine Light.

An epiphany of grace outpoured has cleansed the smudgy windows of her interior self. The illumination of the Divine can now fill the castle and flow through her into the world. Having come to this point in the Seventh Dwelling Places, Teresa no longer finds it necessary to describe in detail the extraordinary phenomena she depicted in the sixth mansions. She returns at this loftiest state to the "little virtues." These comprise the good deeds converted hearts want to do to show their love for God. So changed are they that once formidable obstacles are no longer a hindrance to their living a virtuous life. Whereas locutions, flights, visions, and arrows seem to be miles away from our mostly pedestrian experiences, what the saint has to say of the little virtues or mortifications God asks of us in daily life have a familiar ring about them:

> Certainly, if there were no other gain in this way of prayer except to understand the particular care God has in communicating with us and beseeching us to remain with Him—for this experience doesn't seem to be anything else—it seems to me that all the trials endured for the sake of enjoying these touches of His love, so gentle and penetrating, would be well worthwhile (IC, 185:9).

A reaffirmation like this assures us in the simplest sense that it is acceptable to be absolutely ordinary. We do not have to be perfect to enjoy the intimacy of divine companionship. Jesus wants us to turn our grandiose desires for earthly perfection over to him in genuine admissions of our weakness so that he can be our strength. The soul's delight consists of the fact that she does nothing but that, in and through Christ, all is done. Though the soul may have undergone many trials and afflictions, she is at rest in the tent she shares with Christ. No other love takes precedence in her life. He frees her at one and the same time to be herself and to obey him. As Teresa puts it:

> Every way in which the Lord helps the soul here, and all He teaches it, takes place with such quiet and so noiselessly that, seemingly, the work resembles the building of Solomon's temple where no sound was heard. So in this temple of God, in this His dwelling

> place, He alone and the soul rejoice together in the
> deepest silence. There is no reason for the intellect
> to stir or seek anything, for the Lord who created it
> wishes to give it repose here and that through a small
> crevice it might observe what is taking place. At times
> this sight is lost and the other faculties do not allow the
> intellect to look, but this happens for only a very short
> time. In my opinion, the faculties are not lost here;
> they do not work, but remain as though in amazement
> (IC, 186:11).

Where the soul once had to cope with bouts of agitation, she now dwells in the peace only Christ can give (cf. John 14:27). Arduous tasks are more quickly done. Why waste time worrying about what does not go one's way or lamenting a suffering that comes into one's life that one would prefer to avoid? It is not that the soul represses the awareness of realistic discomforts; it is only that she refuses to be overly concerned about them. Business matters that once preoccupied her and sapped her energy have to be taken in stride but not at the expense of losing her peace and joy. She puts all parts of her life under God's providential care. Another freeing factor concerns the depth of her self-forgetfulness. This virtue looms large because of Christ's presence in her soul. It enables her to attain a greater amount of interior freedom, for every time she decreases Christ increases (cf. John 3:30).

Throughout *The Interior Castle*, Teresa treasures her relationships with her sisters as well as the threads of Providence woven through her own and their history. Precious as the accomplishments of the reform of Carmel might be, not even they are of ultimate importance. God has drawn her to a place of grace that outrivals any person, event, or thing encountered on her journey thus far. The grace of mystical marriage has had another powerful effect on her. It has softened any semblance of judgmentalism and enabled her to accept with equanimity her own and other's weaknesses. She delights in the trials and afflictions God sends. She enjoys the levity of lightheartedness. This gentle lifestyle tempers the enmity linked with envy and jealousy, which so often despoils our relationships. The more we behold the Epiphany of Christ in our own and others' lives, the more this softening of selfism occurs. Ours is no longer an envious "I", but a respectful "I." The "I" of enmity has been replaced by the Christ "I" of compassion, which alerts us to what we can do to make others happy.

This gentling effect also extends to the community to which we belong. We care deeply for those who share our table and live under our roof. The tender love the soul experiences of Jesus for her creates a radiant circle that takes in all other souls, too. In our time a person who witnessed to this love was Mother Teresa of Calcutta. She allowed the compassion of Christ to spread through her to all those entrusted to her care. Another virtue the soul experiences is that of "holy indifference" or equanimity. The cymbal clashes of ecstasy and rapture, with their effects on the senses, fade as softly as a finished symphony. What remains in their wake is a sea of inner stillness at the core of one's being. What is left in the soul is less a remembrance of these ecstatic moments and more an adherence to their Source. God alone is the one to whom she wants to bind herself.

This state of holy equilibrium is more to be trusted than the corporeal communications of a soul seemingly on fire with the Spirit. Thanks to this return to inner peace, one can rest assured that all selfish desires for consolations have been replaced by the selfless bonds of intimacy. One walks with empty hands lifted up to God to whom the initiative for union belongs. Silent music is the soul's best way of speaking to God. "You alone are Holy, you alone are God...Yours is the kingdom, the power, and the glory."

In our own way, all of us long to arrive at this silent center, this hidden hermitage of our heart. We may experience being there in moments of ego-desperation, when we have done all that we could and even then our best efforts tire us to the point where all we want is to hear and obey like a child the guiding whispers of the Holy Spirit. Not the sound of our own voice but the silence of the mystery becomes the main orientation of our soul. Such a happening has staying power. It begins, like a sweet refrain, to pervade every beat of our heart, every breath of our body. We walk in the company of Christ, gentle enough with ourselves and others to fall asleep in his arms. This consummation in love begins to surround and sustain our soul at all times.

The disciples who followed Christ from the moment he called them tried their best to sustain him during his waking hours and keep watch with him during endless nights on the road. They felt mortified when they could not stay awake with him before those agonizing hours of his Crucifixion (cf. Mark 14:32-42). They had yet to learn the secret of absolute abandonment to the mystery and the way it would mellow their hearts. No wonder Saint Teresa saw as a fitting end to her mansions the simple disclosure, told to her sisters, to fix their eyes on the Crucified. She who had attained understanding of the most profound stages of the mystical life of union with the Trinity returns in the end to the humanity of Jesus. What matters for our Christian formation are the character virtues we cultivate and the final turning of our will over to his. Only then can we set our hand to the plow and continue our mission. When our will and God's are one, we are free to serve our Beloved with joy.

The two main lessons Teresa would have us learn from the mansions are these: the total surrender of our will to the Divine Will, and the willingness to let God use us to complete whatever work we are destined by him to do on earth to advance his holy reign here as

in heaven. The will to love and the love of work—sanctity and service—comprise the unbeatable combination Teresa wanted her sisters
and us, her readers, to attain with the help of grace. She was convinced
that in accordance with the degree of grace we received we could say
with Christ, "Yes, Father." We could try to do what the Divine asked
of us in our day-to-day life and pray to reach this conclusion:

> Thus, Sisters, that you might build on good founda-
> tions, strive to be the least and the slaves of all, look-
> ing at how or where you can please and serve them.
> What you do in this matter you do more for yourself
> than for them and lay stones so firmly that the castle
> will not fall (IC, 191:8).

Humility, the capacity to admit our need for God; detachment
from anything in life that prevents us from becoming other Christs;
and mutual love or charity—these are the keys to Christian spirituality.
Teresa's counsel ought never to be far from our heart:

> Fix your eyes on the Crucified and everything will be-
> come small for you. If His Majesty showed us His love
> by means of such works and frightful torments, how is
> it that you want to please Him only with words? Do
> you know what it means to be truly spiritual? It means
> becoming the slaves of God. Marked with His brand,
> which is that of the cross, spiritual persons, because now
> they have given Him their liberty, can be sold by Him
> as slaves of everyone, as He was. He doesn't thereby do
> them any harm or grant them a small favor. And if souls
> aren't determined about becoming His slave, let them
> be convinced that they are not making much progress,
> for this whole building, as I have said, has humility as
> its foundation. If humility is not genuinely present, for
> your own sake the Lord will not construct a high build-
> ing lest that building fall to the ground (IC, 190-191:8).

Such is the beauty and the mystery of the Christian life. Its core revelation is that we are to love God with our whole soul, mind, will, and heart, and to love our neighbor as ourselves. This Great Commandment sounds simple, but it entails the lifelong sacrifice of leaving behind every remnant of selfish sensuality that blocks our way to God. We may fail him, but he never gives up on us. He sends us the grace we need to transform our character in Christ and to free us from sin. This liberation can only come through self-renunciation. Without humility we cannot enter the interior castle nor approach the treasury of divine intimacy awaiting us at its center.

Not surprisingly Teresa ends the mansions with the story of Martha and Mary (cf. Luke 10:38-42). She does not hide the fact that she, a contemplative nun, is also a Martha, doing her daily tasks and finding in them not only satisfaction but sanctification. Her mission is to bring souls to sit at his feet so that all may be saved and praise him forever. The Mary in her honors this side of Christ's call. Both aspects of full Christian personhood operate in rhythm with one another: the love-will typical of Mary and the work-will typical of Martha:

> In sum, my Sisters, what I conclude with is that we shouldn't build castles in the air. The Lord doesn't look so much at the greatness of our works as at the love with which they are done. And if we do what we can, His Majesty will enable us each day to do more and more, provided that we do not quickly tire. But during the little while this life lasts—and perhaps it will last a shorter time than each one thinks—let us offer the Lord interiorly and exteriorly the sacrifice we can. His Majesty will join it with that which He offered on the cross to the Father for us. Thus even though our works are small they will have the value our love for Him would have merited had they been great (IC, 194:15).

Obviously, Teresa of Avila has been given the grace to convey to the whole Church, to all Christians and people of good will, the foundations of formative spirituality. The Gospel story comes alive again in her words and through her experiences. It captures our heart and encourages us to live in Christ-like presence, day after day, without being discouraged. Thanks to these Teresian teachings and the practical counsels they embody, we can resonate with the full and freeing truth that "God alone suffices."

Recommended Reading

Auclair, Marcelle. *Saint Teresa of Avila*. New York, NY: Pantheon Books, 1953.

Bouyer, Louis. *Women Mystics: Hadewijch of Antwerp, Teresa of Avila, Thérèse of Lisieux, Elizabeth of the Trinity, Edith Stein*. Trans. Anne Englund Nash. San Francisco, CA: Ignatius Press, 1993.

Medwick, Cathleen. *Teresa of Avila. The Progress of a Soul*. New York, NY: Knopf, 1999.

McGinn, Bernard. *The Flowering of Mysticism*. New York, NY: Crossroad Publishing Co., 1998.

McLean, Julienne. *Towards Mystical Union*. New York, NY: St. Pauls Publishing, 2003.

Muto, Susan. *A Practical Guide to Spiritual Reading*. Petersham, MA: St. Bede's Publications, 1994.

————. *Dear Master: Letters on Spiritual Direction Inspired by Saint John of the Cross*. A Companion to *The Living Flame of Love*. Liguori, MO: Liguori Publications, 1999.

————. *Deep Into the Thicket: Soul Searching Meditations Inspired by The Spiritual Canticle of Saint John of the Cross*. Pittsburgh, PA: Epiphany Books, 2001.

————. "Inquiry as a Spiritual Quest: Teresa as Guide." *Spiritual Life*. Volume 49, Number 1, Spring 2003, 44-52.

————. *John of the Cross for Today: The Ascent*. Pittsburgh, PA: Epiphany Books, 1998.

————. *John of the Cross for Today: The Dark Night.* Pittsburgh, PA: Epiphany Books, 2000.

————. *Late Have I Loved Thee: The Recovery of Intimacy.* New York, NY: Crossroad, 1995.

————. *Pathways of Spiritual Living.* Petersham, MA: St. Bede's Publications, 1988.

————. "Reconciling Sanctity and Service–The Perfect Way of Saint Teresa of Avila." *Carmelite Digest.* Volume 18, No. 4, Fall 2003, 10-21.

Teresa of Avila, Saint. *The Book of Her Life* in *The Collected Works.* Volume One, Trans. Kieran Kavanaugh and Otilio Rodriguez. Washington, DC: ICS Publications, 1980.

————. *The Book of Her Life* in *The Collected Works.* Volume Two. Trans. Kieran Kavanaugh, and Otilio Rodriguez. DC: ICS Publications, 1980.

————. *The Collected Works.* Volume 2. Trans. Kieran Kavanaugh and Otilio Rodriguez. Washington, DC: ICS Publications, 1980.

————. *The Way of Perfection* in *The Collected Works.* Volume One. Trans. Kieran Kavanaugh and Otilio Rodriguez. Second Ed. Rev. Washington, DC: ICS Publications, 1987.

————. *The Way of Perfection* in *The Collected Works.* Volume Two. Trans. Kieran Kavanaugh and Otilio Rodriguez. Second Ed. Rev. Washington, DC: ICS Publications. 1987.

————. *The Way of Perfection.* (A Study Edition.) Trans. Kieran Kavanaugh and Otilio Rodriguez. Washington, DC: ICS Publications, 2000.

————. *The Collected Letters.* Volume One. Trans Kieran Kavanaugh. Washington, DC: ICS Publications, 2001.

Teresa of Avila: The Interior Castle in *The Classics of Western Spirituality.* Trans. Kieran Kavanagh, O.C.D. and Otilio Rodriguez, O.C.D. New York, NY: Paulist Press, 1979.

The Collected Works of Saint John of the Cross. Trans. Kieran Kavanaugh, OCD and Otilio Rodriques, OCD. Washington, DC: ICS Publications, 1991.

The Soul's Passion for God: Selected Writings of Teresa of Avila. Ed. Keith Beasley-Topliffe. Nashville, TN: Upper Room Books, 1997.

The Institute of Carmelite Studies promotes research and publication in the field of Carmelite spirituality. Its members are Discalced Carmelites, part of a Roman Catholic community—friars, nuns, and laity—who are heirs to the teaching and way of life of Teresa of Jesus and John of the Cross, men and women dedicated to contemplation and to ministry in the Church and the world. Information concerning their way of life is available through local diocesan Vocation Offices or from the Vocation Directors' Offices:

1233 So. 45th Street, W. Milwaukee, WI 53214

P.O. Box 3420, San Jose, CA 95156-3420

5151 Marylake Drive, Little Rock, AR 72206